# God Favors the Fool

Elena Olympia Collins

# Discover the Tarot as Never Seen Before

From the acclaimed author Elena Olympia Collins comes **Tarot Well Done** – a groundbreaking exploration that goes beyond intuition and into the structured language of the Rider-Waite tarot deck.

Praised for its depth, clarity, and originality, Collins demystifies tarot by revealing the symbolism, color theory, and numerical patterns that form the foundation of every reading. With close to 40 years of expertise, she challenges traditional approaches, encouraging readers to see tarot as a language rather than just a divination tool.

Described as thought-provoking and meticulously researched, **Tarot Well Done** offers a fresh perspective for both beginners and seasoned practitioners alike. It's a book that has reshaped the way readers interpret the cards – unlocking a structured, reliable, and deeply insightful approach to tarot reading.

Whether you're new to tarot or seeking a more profound understanding, this book will illuminate the path.

Join the journey. Challenge the narrative. **Read Tarot Well Done.**

Find **Tarot Well Done** at all great booksellers and libraries across the world. Available in Paperback, Hardback, Large-print, eBook and Audiobook.

# Table of Contents

# Preface

## From Foundations to Elevation

Every book begins with a question.

My first book, *Tarot Well Done*, asked: How can tarot be understood clearly, practically, and without unhelpful mystification? It was written to give readers a solid foundation – a way to approach the cards with confidence, to see their symbolic language as accessible, and to use them as tools for reflection rather than superstition. That book was about clarity, structure, and the practical art of reading tarot well.

This book, *God Favors the Fool*, begins with a different question: What does tarot reveal about the deeper journey of human growth and consciousness itself? If *Tarot Well Done* was about learning the language, this book is about entering the conversation. It is a companion volume, designed to take you beyond the mechanics of reading tarot and into the transformative wisdom the cards embody. Where the first book explored meanings and methods, this one turns to the architecture of the Fool's Journey – a way of seeing human development through the lens of archetypes. The Fool's Journey offers a map – not of fortune, but of development.

The title reflects this shift. I do not see God as a distant figure in the sky, but as the universal consciousness in which we are immersed. The more we expand our awareness, the more God-like we become – not in the sense of power, but in the sense of wholeness. The Fool is favored not because of innocence, but because of willingness – the willingness to step forward, to risk, to grow.

The Fool's journey is our journey, and the destination is not external but internal: the awakening of consciousness, the integration of self, the embodiment of wholeness.

This book is structured to guide you through that journey. Each chapter begins with a Major Arcana archetype, paired with its Minor Arcana counterparts. From there, the chapter explores how this pairing reflects a stage of human development. Archetypes emerge from the spiritual and psychological layers of human development, but they do not stay contained there. Each chapter follows the natural ripple that moves outward once an archetype is activated, drawing connections to emotions, relationships, culture, creativity, science, and myth.

You'll see how the language of tarot resonates with wisdom traditions across time and place, how inner patterns become outer behaviors. Tarot will reveal itself as an open language of growth rather than a closed system of symbols – each card an expression of the interwoven fabric of psychology, mythology, cosmology, and science.

In this way, *God Favors the Fool* takes you to the next level. If *Tarot Well Done* gave you the tools to read the cards, this book gives you the framework to live them. It moves from interpretation to integration, from definition to transformation. It shows how tarot is intended to take the reader beyond simply understanding symbols and into the realm of embodying consciousness. It is more than reading cards – it is about reading yourself, your culture, your history, and your future. It is about life.

You will also find journaling prompts at the end of each chapter. These are not exercises in prediction, but invitations to reflection. They are designed to help you integrate the archetype into your own life, to see how the stage of growth described in the chapter is unfolding in your own journey. It is a message to you – about your growth, your healing, your awakening.

Writing this book has been both challenging and rewarding. It has required me to confront my own assumptions, to integrate my own experiences, and to expand my own awareness. It has reminded me that growth is not linear, but cyclical. It has reminded me that endings are beginnings, that collapse is renewal, that shadow is the doorway to light. It has reminded me that God favors the Fool, because the Fool fearlessly steps into the unknown.

My hope is that this book will serve as a companion on your journey. I have written it with the belief that the archetypal characters and themes appearing in the imagery were intended to decipher the human condition rather than prompt psychic predictions. They express, with exquisite clarity, our enduring spirit and the psychological patterns we live within. They showcase the unspoken depth and breadth of our individual and collective potential.

If *Tarot Well Done* was your introduction to the language of tarot, *God Favors the Fool* is your invitation to speak it fluently, to live it deeply, and to embody its wisdom.

Whether you are new to tarot or have studied it for years; whether you approach it as a spiritual practice or a psychological tool; whether you see it as art, myth, or language, I hope you will find in these pages something that resonates – a mirror of your own growth, a map of your own journey, and an invitation to your own awakening.

This is not a book to be read once and set aside. It is a book to be lived with, reflected on, and returned to. It is a book that grows as you grow, that speaks differently as you change, that mirrors your journey as it unfolds. It is a book that reminds you that you are the Fool, that you are favored, that you are becoming.

# Introduction

## Why God Favors the Fool

*"The Fool's Journey is not a tale of fortune-telling, but a mirror of human becoming. Each step along the path – whether guided by archetypal figures or tested by life's adversities – reveals that tarot is less a deck of predictions than a language of growth. To walk with the Fool is to walk with ourselves: to stumble, to learn, to transform, and to discover that what begins in innocence ends in wisdom. Tarot, at its heart, is the story of how we grow into wholeness."*

*— Elena Olympia Collins*

My own learning has never been a straight line. I moved forward, doubled back, and circled through the same lessons more than once. Some patterns only revealed themselves after I had lived them repeatedly. It was the discipline of learning tarot at a high level that finally helped me recognize those patterns — the ones that shape who we are and how we move through the world. Tarot taught me to see beyond the moment, to notice the cycles and systems that repeat through every life, every relationship, every challenge. It became the language through which I learned to understand the deeper architecture of experience.

To set the tone for what follows, let's get my take on the 'God' part clarified early. To speak of God is to speak of consciousness. Not a distant ruler in the sky, nor a figure demanding worship, but the living presence of awareness itself. God is the word we use to describe the universal field of being – the infinite source from which all life arises, and to which all life returns.

Human development is the path by which we draw closer to this source. Each moment of growth, each act of courage, each surrender to truth expands our conscious awareness. In doing so, we become more God-like – not in the sense of power or dominion, but in the sense of wholeness, integration, and love. The Fool's journey through tarot is the mirror of this path: a cycle of innocence, challenge, shadow, renewal, and completion. It is the story of becoming.

## The Origins of "God"

To understand God is to first understand where the word itself comes from. The term did not originate in the Bible, nor in any single religious text. Its roots lie in the Early Bronze Age, a time of immense cultural and technological development: agriculture, animal domestication, and the first metal tools.

It was tied to daily rituals and was an expression of invocation — a way to bring attention to something in the environment that must transform, grow, or yield reward. It was a word of gratitude, of blessing, of calling forth change. In this sense, the word was not about a distant deity, but about the human capacity to invoke transformation.

Over centuries, as languages evolved and scriptures were translated, the original Hebrew names in the Bible – Elohim, Yahweh, Adonai, El Shaddai, Elyon – simply became "God." But in its truest form, God is invocation, transformation, the human ability to call forth growth. To say "God" is to acknowledge our own role in creation, our own power to invoke change. Our human potential.

In this sense, God is not separate from us. God is us, when we shift perspective and recognize that consciousness itself is divine.

## The Self as Sacred

Psychology teaches us that the self is layered – conscious and unconscious, instinct and intuition, shadow and light. We feel these layers in moments of conflict, longing, intuition, or fear. Spirituality teaches us that these layers are not obstacles, but gateways. To know the self is to know the divine, for the self is the vessel through which universal consciousness flows.

When we confront our fears, we expand awareness. When we integrate shadow, we reclaim wholeness. When we cultivate compassion, we embody God. The Fool reminds us that the self is not static – it is a process, a journey, a continual unfolding toward greater consciousness.

## Spirituality as Growth

Spirituality is often mistaken for belief, ritual, or worship. In truth, it is a sense of self – an inner orientation, rather than anything outward-facing. We experience it in moments of clarity, connection, awe, or quiet recognition. It is growth. It is the expansion of awareness beyond the ego, beyond the illusion of separateness, into the recognition that all life is interconnected.

Tarot, psychology, meditation, prophecy, and myth are all languages of this growth. They are maps of consciousness, guiding us through the terrain of human experience. Each archetype, each symbol, each story reflects the universal truth: that we are fragments of God, learning to remember our wholeness.

# Psychology as Path

Modern psychology speaks of individuation – the lifelong process of integrating all aspects of the self into a unified whole. This is not separate from spirituality; it is its practical expression. Individuation is awakening made tangible. It is the slow, courageous work of becoming who we truly are.

We experience this path in the most human ways: healing trauma, regulating emotion, learning to tell the truth, and choosing actions that align with our values. Each step clears space for consciousness to shine more fully through us. Growth becomes less about striving and more about remembering.

The Fool's journey mirrors this psychological unfolding. Strength becomes emotional regulation. Temperance becomes integration. The Devil becomes shadow confrontation. The Tower becomes collapse. The Star becomes renewal. The Moon becomes discernment. The Sun becomes vitality. Judgement becomes awakening. The World becomes wholeness.

Psychology and tarot converge in the same truth: healing is transformation, and transformation is divine.

# The Infinite Search

The search for God is not a search for a distant being – it is the lifelong turning inward toward wholeness. It is the daily practice of expanding awareness, of softening the ego, of remembering that separation is an illusion.

We experience this search in quiet, human ways: in moments of honesty, in the courage to face our own patterns, in the tenderness that arises when we see ourselves clearly. Growth is not a leap into perfection but a steady unfolding into deeper presence.

We do not become God by worshiping an external figure. We become God by embodying consciousness — by living with compassion, integrating shadow, and surrendering to truth. The Fool's journey reminds us that every ending is a beginning, every collapse is renewal, every shadow is a doorway to light.

The goal is not to reach perfection, but to remember our wholeness. To become, as fully as we can in this lifetime, a clear expression of the divine consciousness that moves through all things.

## Invitation to the Reader

This book is not a manual of fortune-telling. It is a map of growth, a mirror of consciousness, a guide to the ongoing journey of becoming. Tarot serves here as a symbolic language for exploring that path, not as a tool for prediction. The destination is universal: the expansion of awareness, the healing of the self, the integration of shadow, and the embodiment of wholeness.

You are the Fool, stepping into the journey. You are the seeker, striving for consciousness. You are the fragment of God, remembering your wholeness.

# The Language of the Journey
## The Fool's Archetypal Journal of Growth

Human beings have always searched for maps – not only to navigate the world, but to understand themselves. We draw them on cave walls, carve them into stone, sketch them in journals, and trace them in memory. A map gives us orientation. It tells us where we are, where we have been, and where we might go next.

The tarot is one such map. It does not chart geography, but consciousness. It traces the inner terrain of growth, shadow, awakening, and return. When we follow the Fool's path through the cards, we are not learning a system – we are learning ourselves.

This book is structured as a journey because human development is not linear. It spirals, deepens, repeats, and expands. Each chapter reveals a stage of growth, expressed through the archetypal language of the Major Arcana and reflected in the everyday experiences of the Minor suits. The cards are not the destination; they are the signposts. They point toward truths spoken across cultures, centuries, and wisdom traditions. They remind us that human development is not a solitary pursuit, but part of a universal pattern.

More specifically, this book is structured to show you how tarot's symbolic language mirrors the stages of psychological growth and spiritual awakening. Each chapter begins with a single archetype and explores how its imagery connects to the Minor Arcana, to the elemental suits, and to the lived experience of being human. The cards speak not only of personal development, but of collective evolution. Their patterns echo wisdom found in philosophy, religion, science, and myth. When viewed this way, ancient messages – including scripture and prophecy – become easier to understand as reflections of recurring archetypal patterns that shape human experience across cultures and across time.

I have chosen this structure to invite you into a conversation, rather than imply any strict memorization or interpretation of meaning. Tarot is a language, and like any language, it is alive. It adapts, evolves, and resonates differently depending on who is speaking and who is listening. By pairing each Major Arcana stage with its Minor Arcana counterparts, we create a framework that is both consistent and expansive. It allows us to see how the grand archetypes of human growth are reflected in the everyday experiences of creativity, emotion, intellect, and material life.

You will notice that each chapter does more than describe a card. It draws connections. It shows how the imagery of tarot aligns with psychological theories of development, with spiritual practices of discernment, with cultural traditions of storytelling, and with scientific insights into human behavior. This is intentional. Tarot is not isolated from the rest of human knowledge; it is a mirror of it. When we read the cards, we are not only reading symbols – we are reading ourselves, as we were, as we are, and as we may strive to be.

The journey you are about to take is therefore both ancient and modern. It is ancient because the archetypes of tarot echo myths, prophecies, and rituals that have guided humanity for millennia. It is modern because we now have the tools of psychology, the sciences, and cultural analysis to understand these archetypes in new ways. It is cosmic because it reminds us that our growth is not confined to earthly concerns but is part of a larger unfolding of consciousness.

This transitional chapter is here to prepare you for that journey. It is here to remind you that what follows is not a series of isolated lessons, but a coherent path. Each chapter builds on the last, and together they form a cycle of growth. The Fool's journey is the spine of the book, but the richness comes from the connections we draw to other wisdoms. You will encounter insights from Jungian psychology, from ancient prophecies, from modern science, from cultural traditions, and from spiritual practices. Each of these will illuminate the cards in new ways, showing that tarot is not a closed system, but an open language.

It is important to understand that this book does not ask you to believe in tarot as a supernatural tool. It asks you to see tarot as a symbolic language that helps us understand ourselves and the larger story we belong to. The cards are not fortune-telling devices; they are mirrors. They reflect to us the stages of development we all experience, the challenges we all face, and the possibilities we all hold. By learning this language, we gain a map of our own journey. We gain a way to understand ourselves and the world around us.

It has been a painstaking tightrope walk to create a book that is not only about tarot, or even about how tarot aligns with psychology or spirituality. It is a book about life in all its forms. It is about how we grow, how we heal, how we integrate, and how we awaken. It is about the movement from innocence to mastery, from shadow to light, from collapse to renewal, from individuality to wholeness. It is about how we become more God-like. Not in the sense of power, but in the sense of consciousness.

As you move through the chapters, you will see that the journey is both personal and collective, and that the tightrope is sturdier than it first appears. It is personal because each of us must walk our own path, confront our own shadows, and embrace our own growth. It is collective because the archetypes are universal.

They speak to experiences shared across culture, religion, and era. They remind us that we belong to a larger story, an unfolding of consciousness that connects us all.

This book is therefore both a guide and an invitation. The chapters ahead will challenge you, inspire you, and invite you to see tarot in new ways. They will show you that tarot is not about predicting the future but about understanding the present. They will show you that tarot is not about external authority, but about personal and collective growth – and the inner and outer transformations that emerge within that growth. They will show you that tarot is not about superstition, but about consciousness.

By the time you reach the end of the book, you will see that the Fool's journey is not only the structure of tarot, but the structure of life. You will see that the archetypes are not only symbols, but mirrors. You will see that the language of tarot is not only about cards, but about consciousness. You will see that God favors the Fool, because the Fool is willing to step into the journey, to grow, to awaken, and to become.

Take a moment to pause and recognize that you are standing at the threshold. The preface and introduction have set the stage, and this chapter has given you the language you'll need to navigate what follows. It is the reminder that the journey ahead is not random, but structured. It is the invitation to see tarot as a language of growth, and to see yourself as the traveller on the path.

The next chapter will show you how to walk it.

# How to Use This Book

## Orientation

This book is an invitation to recognize your own patterns. It offers archetypes, psychological insights, and spiritual principles, but it does not ask you to adopt a belief system. It asks you to pay attention. You can read it in order, or you can move intuitively. Both paths are valid.

### Reading the Chapters

Each chapter explores a Major Arcana card through three intertwined lenses: psychological development, spiritual principle, and universal pattern. These lenses braid together. As you read, notice which one speaks most clearly to you. Let your attention follow what feels alive.

### Working With the Journal Prompts

The prompts are invitations, not tasks. They exist to help you recognize your own patterns, integrate insights into lived experience, and track your growth over time. The form doesn't matter. The moment of self-contact does.

## Using the Book for Self-Reflection

This book is not a diagnostic tool. It is a companion for reflection. You can return to certain cards during specific seasons of life:

- ❖ when you're beginning something new

- ❖ when you're navigating conflict

- ❖ when you're integrating lessons

- ❖ when you're closing a chapter

Let the cards meet you where you are. Let the reflections help you name what is shifting. Let the patterns remind you that growth is cyclical, not linear.

## The Spark We Share

There is a thread running through this book that is older than tarot and deeper than doctrine: the spark of human potential survives every forgetting. It is the part of us that endures beneath fear, distortion, distraction, and collapse. It is the quiet intelligence that keeps reaching for clarity even when the world teaches confusion.

Some call it soul. Some call it consciousness. Some call it God. But whatever name we give it, the spark is human. It lives in our capacity to imagine, to choose, to change, to create, to repair, to remember. It is not bestowed from above; it is carried from within.

The Rider-Waite imagery hints at this. The psychology names it. The spiritual principles honor it. The mythic patterns reveal it. And this book asks you to recognize it in yourself — not as an abstract ideal, but as a living possibility.

When you read this book, you are not just learning the cards. You are learning to see the spark in your own life. And when you share what you see — through conversation, reflection, or simple presence — you help ignite the collective potential that has always been waiting.

## A Living Journey

You will not read this book the same way twice. As you change, the cards change. As you grow, the meanings deepen. This is the nature of archetypes – they evolve as you do.

When one person remembers their spark, the collective brightens. And there is a particular kind of thrill in being among the early knowers — the ones who notice the pattern before it becomes common knowledge, who sense that the world is more malleable than it appears, who understand that co-creation begins not with institutions but with individuals who can see clearly.

To read this book with that awareness is to recognize a near-secret hiding in plain sight: that human potential is not theoretical, not symbolic, not aspirational. It is active. It is waiting. It is one choice away. And those who learn to work with it — through attention, reflection, and the courage to see themselves honestly — become the first sparks in a field that is already primed to ignite.

When you step into the Fool's chapter, you are not just beginning a journey. You are joining the small but growing circle of people who understand that a new world is not built by force, but by recognition — one spark at a time.

Turn the page and begin.

# The Fool and the Pages

## Beginnings, Curiosity, and the Language of Growth

*"The journey has just begun, and so far, the load is light. It is time to move forward from zero, relying on instinct. The path of a lifetime awaits you and as you step toward your destiny there will be choices to make, each of which takes you one step closer to a positive or negative outcome. This is only the first of these choices, and the choice is yours."*

*– Excerpt from Tarot Well Done*

## The Fool as Zero: The Blank Slate

The Fool begins the journey at zero. Zero is not nothing – it is potential. It is the space before definition, the openness that allows anything to emerge. In developmental psychology, this stage is often described as infancy: a time when the self is not yet formed, when experience is absorbed without judgment. The

Fool is impressionable, fearless, and unaware of danger. He steps forward without baggage, without the weight of past choices, and without the limits of learned caution.

This openness is both a gift and a risk. It allows for spontaneity, creativity, and trust in life. But it also leaves the Fool vulnerable to distraction, poor judgment, or naivety. The Fool's naivety is not a flaw but a form of sacred openness – the willingness to step forward without certainty, which is the beginning of all learning. In spiritual traditions, this stage is often seen as the "beginner's mind" – a state of receptivity that Zen Buddhism values as the foundation of wisdom.

In psychology, it mirrors the early developmental stage where curiosity drives learning, but boundaries and discernment are not yet established. In neuroscience, this openness mirrors the brain's early plasticity – a period when neural pathways are rapidly forming, pruning, and reorganizing in response to experience. The Fool's zero is not emptiness, but a field of possibility shaped by curiosity and encounter.

## The Pages: Four Faces of Youthful Potential

The Minor Arcana Pages mirror the Fool's innocence. Each Page represents a youthful archetype within its suit – Wands, Cups, Swords, and Pentacles. Across cultures, youth is often portrayed as the age of messengers, apprentices, and initiates. It is the youthful who carry new ideas into the world before tradition has fully shaped them. The four Pages of tarot are messengers, learners, and explorers. Together, they show how the Fool's openness expresses itself in different domains of life: creativity, emotion, thought, and material reality.

## Page of Wands: Enthusiasm and Autonomy

The Page of Wands stands in a barren landscape, gazing upward at the budding wand in his hand. His message is one of enthusiasm, encouragement, and limitless potential. He represents the free spirit who trusts inspiration and believes in possibilities greater than his current circumstances.

Psychologically, this Page reflects the developmental stage of autonomy – the child who begins to explore the world independently, driven by curiosity and imagination. Spiritually, he embodies the fire of creativity, the spark that says, "I can try." His optimism is vital, but it can also lead to overestimation or immaturity. The barren desert reminds us that enthusiasm alone is not enough; it must be grounded in reality.

Developmental research shows that early autonomy is fueled by the brain's reward system, which lights up when children explore, imagine, and test their independence. Many cultures celebrate this spark through rites of passage that honor the first steps toward selfhood.

## Page of Cups: Emotional Curiosity and Self-Discovery

The Page of Cups holds a chalice with a fish peeking out, symbolizing creativity, intuition, and emotional insight. His message is one of playfulness, openness, and the invitation to be true to oneself. He represents the youthful heart that remains curious about identity, relationships, and feelings.

In psychology, this Page resonates with the stage of emotional development where children begin to understand themselves as individuals with unique feelings and identities. The fish, often linked to faith and fertility, reminds us of the abundance that comes from emotional openness. Spiritually, the Page of Cups invites us to celebrate our inner life, to remain youthful at heart, and to embrace creativity as a path to authenticity.

Studies in emotional development show that children learn who they are by mirroring and being mirrored – a process that shapes identity, empathy, and intuition. Many cultural traditions recognize this stage as the awakening of the heart, where imagination and feeling become guides.

## Page of Swords: Mental Agility and Experimentation

The Page of Swords stands alert on a windy hilltop, sword raised, ready to test ideas. His message is one of mental agility, restlessness, and the challenge to stagnant thought. He represents the youthful mind that experiments, questions, and sometimes shocks others with new perspectives.

Psychologically, this Page reflects cognitive development – the stage where curiosity about ideas leads to experimentation, debate, and sometimes rebellion. Spiritually, he embodies the air element: the restless wind that clears clouds or gathers them. His energy reminds us that growth requires testing boundaries, even at the risk of conflict. The Page of Swords teaches that ideas are powerful tools, but they must be wielded with care.

Cognitive science describes this stage as the emergence of executive function – the ability to plan, question, and experiment. In many societies, this is the age when children begin to challenge norms, a necessary step in forming independent thought.

## Page of Pentacles: Practical Curiosity and Material Beginnings

The Page of Pentacles gazes intently at the coin he holds, standing in a field of grass and flowers. His message is one of curiosity, learning, and the prospect of tangible growth. He represents the youthful drive to study, to cultivate skills, and to build a foundation for prosperity.

In psychology, this Page reflects the stage of practical learning – studentship, discipline, and the slow accumulation of knowledge. Spiritually, he embodies the earth element: grounded, steady, and ambitious. His coin is not just wealth, but potential – the reminder that dreams can become reality through effort and persistence. The Page of Pentacles teaches that material success begins with curiosity and commitment.

Anthropologists note that nearly every culture introduces young people to practical skills through imitation, repetition, and hands-on learning. The Page of Pentacles reflects this universal stage of grounded apprenticeship.

## The Fool and the Pages Together

The Fool and the Pages together form the foundation of the tarot's developmental language. The Fool is the blank slate, the openness to life. The Pages are the first expressions of that openness in specific domains:

* **Wands (Fire)**: Creative enthusiasm and autonomy.

* **Cups (Water)**: Emotional curiosity and self-discovery.

* **Swords (Air)**: Mental agility and experimentation.

* **Pentacles (Earth)**: Practical curiosity and material beginnings.

Together, they show that growth begins with innocence, curiosity, and the willingness to explore. Each Page is a messenger, reminding us that the Fool's journey is not just mythic – it is lived daily in our creativity, emotions, thoughts, and practical pursuits.

# Psychological and Spiritual Resonance

From a psychological perspective, the Fool and the Pages represent early developmental stages: openness, curiosity, experimentation, and learning. They remind us that growth begins with play, exploration, and the willingness to risk failure. This psychological foundation naturally opens into the spiritual dimension, because the qualities that support early development also support awakening.

From a spiritual perspective, the Fool and the Pages embody the beginner's mind, the openness to possibility, and the trust that life itself is a teacher. Where psychology describes the mechanics of early growth, spirituality describes its meaning — the sense that innocence is not naïveté but a form of inner alignment.

The Fool's innocence is not something to be outgrown – it is something to be carried forward. Maturity does not replace innocence; it learns how to carry it wisely. The Pages remind us that youthful curiosity is the seed of wisdom. To remain open, curious, and willing to learn is to honor the Fool within us, even as we grow into maturity.

Across cultures, this movement from innocence to initiation appears again and again, revealing that the psychological and spiritual layers of the Fool's journey are part of a much older pattern. Myths across the world echo the Fool's first steps – stories where innocence becomes initiation, and where the untested youth is invited into a larger world.

## Pwyll's Story – Welsh Mythology

The story of Pwyll begins in a quiet forest at dawn, when the young ruler wanders beyond the edges of his own land. Mist hangs low over the ground. The air is still. Then he hears it — the low, rhythmic growl of hounds unlike any he has ever known. Their coats are white as bone, their ears red as embers. They circle a fallen stag, their presence unmistakably otherworldly.

Unaware of the sacredness of the moment, Pwyll drives them away and claims the kill for himself. The forest seems to hold its breath.

Moments later, a figure steps from the shadows: Arawn, the king of the Otherworld. His voice is calm, but the weight of his realm sits behind every word. Instead of punishing Pwyll, he offers him something unexpected – a chance to learn. Arawn proposes an exchange: Pwyll will spend a year and a day in Annwn, ruling in his place. He will wear the king's face, sit on the king's throne, and meet the tests that come with power. Pwyll agrees. He steps into the unknown with no preparation, no training, and no guarantees.

Annwn is not a place he understands. Its nights are deeper, its silences heavier, its challenges sharper. During his year and a day in the Otherworld, Pwyll learns restraint when anger would be easier. He learns humility when pride calls to him. He learns discernment when illusion tempts him. He faces conflict and chooses courage. He faces uncertainty and chooses truth. He faces temptation and chooses integrity.

By the time he returns to his own world, he is no longer the untested youth who stumbled across the hounds in the forest. He earns his title without mastery, but with willingness to learn his way through experience.

Pwyll's story teaches us that openness is what allows us to enter new territory without knowing the rules or the risks. His lack of preconceptions becomes his strength. Because he never assumes he knows, he becomes teachable. His innocence is the very quality that allows him to say yes.

In his year as king of the Otherworld, he learns by doing — mistakes and all. His curiosity allows him to embody the experience rather than recite it from doctrine. He returns wiser not because he sought wisdom, but because he remained open to life's instruction.

Pwyll's story is one in which innocence becomes a spiritual asset. The early stages of learning – the awkwardness, the uncertainty, the mistakes – are not obstacles to wisdom. They are the very material wisdom is made from.

Just like the Fool and the Pages, Pwyll shows us that curiosity is a form of courage, mistakes are stepping stones toward knowledge, humility is the gateway to power, and the willingness to step into the unknown is the first act of every hero.

## Closing Reflection

The Fool steps forward at zero, carrying no baggage. The Pages echo his innocence in four domains of life, showing how openness becomes creativity, emotion, thought, and material growth. Together, they remind us that beginnings are sacred. Every journey starts with curiosity, and every step forward is a choice.

Modern research shows that curiosity is one of the strongest predictors of lifelong learning, adaptability, and resilience — qualities the Fool and the Pages embody from the very beginning. The Fool and the Pages teach us that growth is not about knowing everything — it is about being willing to learn.

## Journaling prompt

*Where in your life are you being invited to step forward with openness, even if you feel uncertain?*

# The Magician and the Aces

## Manifestation, Beginnings, and the Power of Choice

*"You are the conduit of energy which you draw beneath you from the earth, and above you from heaven. It is a time for action and your opportunity to transform. Harness your skills and step confidently into the power you possess. Beware of tricksters, manipulators, and repetitive cycles."*

*– Excerpt from Tarot Well Done*

## The Magician as Number One: The Spark of Manifestation

The Magician is the first numbered card in the Major Arcana. He follows the Fool's innocence with a surge of awareness: the realization that he can act, create, and shape outcomes. His posture — one hand pointing to the heavens, the other to the earth — marks him as a conduit between the spiritual and material realms. He channels energy, but he is also tempted by ego's early illusions. His ability is real, but it is not yet tempered by wisdom.

In developmental psychology, this stage mirrors the emergence of agency. A child begins to realize they can influence their environment — through words, actions, or creativity. Spiritually, the Magician represents the moment when inspiration becomes manifestation. He is the archetype of "I can, and I want to see what happens when I do" – the spark that turns possibility into reality.

## The Aces: Raw Potential in Four Elements

The Minor Arcana Aces mirror the Magician's archetype. Each Ace is the seed of its suit, the raw potential waiting to be harnessed. Together, they show how the Magician's power expresses itself in creativity, emotion, intellect, and material reality.

### Ace of Wands: Inspired Beginnings

A hand emerges from a cloud, offering a wand with budding leaves. The Ace of Wands represents inspiration, passion, and the rush of energy that comes with a new idea. It is the fire of creativity, the impulse to act without overthinking.

Psychologically, this card reflects the spark of motivation — the moment when we feel compelled to try something new. Spiritually, it is the flame of divine inspiration, reminding us that beginnings are sacred but must be grounded in foresight. The falling leaves hint at both abundance and the risk of impulsivity. The Magician channels this fire into action, but without balance, it can burn too quickly.

## Ace of Cups: Emotional Wholeness

A chalice overflows with water as a dove descends, symbolizing love, compassion, and spiritual connection. The Ace of Cups represents the ultimate emotional truth: that many beginnings are rooted in love. It is the water of life, the invitation to open the heart.

Psychologically, this card reflects the development of emotional awareness — the ability to feel, connect, and value oneself. Spiritually, it is the reminder that love is both given and received, and that wholeness comes from embracing both. The Magician channels this water into relationships and creativity, but he must beware of illusions or routine acts of love that lack authenticity.

## Ace of Swords: Clarity and Truth

A hand raises a sword crowned with victory, symbolizing intellect, justice, and revelation. The Ace of Swords represents the triumph of thought — the power of clarity to cut through confusion. It is the air of intellect, the sharpness of communication.

Psychologically, this card reflects cognitive development — the ability to reason, analyze, and articulate truth. Spiritually, it is the sword of discernment, reminding us that clarity can liberate but also wound. The Magician channels this air into ideas and decisions, but he must beware of manipulation or the temptation to wield clarity as a weapon.

**Ace of Pentacles: Material Opportunity**

A hand offers a coin above a cultivated garden, symbolizing prosperity, health, and tangible gifts. The Ace of Pentacles represents the manifestation of material opportunity — the earth of stability and growth. It is the promise of abundance, the seed of practical success.

Psychologically, this card reflects the stage of learning to build — developing skills, cultivating discipline, and creating security. Spiritually, it is the reminder that material gifts can be blessings or distractions, depending on how they are used. The Magician channels this earth into manifestation, but he must beware of greed or corruption.

# The Magician and the Aces Together

The Magician's table holds all four suits: wand, cup, sword, and pentacle. The Aces show the raw potential of each element, waiting to be harnessed. Together, they form a complete picture of manifestation:

- **Wands (Fire)**: Inspiration and creative energy.

- **Cups (Water)**: Emotional wholeness and love.

- **Swords (Air)**: Clarity and intellectual power.

- **Pentacles (Earth)**: Material opportunity and stability.

The Magician teaches that manifestation is not about having one tool — it is about integrating all four. To act without love is reckless. To love without clarity is blind. To think without grounding is unstable. To build without inspiration is empty. The Magician's lesson is that true manifestation requires balance across all domains.

# Psychological and Spiritual Resonance

From a psychological perspective, the Magician and the Aces represent the emergence of agency — the realization that we can act, create, and shape outcomes. They mark the moment when a person first recognizes their capacity to influence their environment. This psychological awakening naturally opens into the spiritual dimension, because the ability to act is inseparable from the awareness that we participate in something larger than ourselves.

From a spiritual perspective, the Magician and the Aces embody the principle of co-creation: the idea that we are not passive observers of life, but collaborators with the creative forces that move through it. Where psychology describes the development of agency, spirituality describes the meaning of that agency — the recognition that creation is not only possible, but sacred.

The Magician reminds us that power is not neutral — it can be used for growth or for manipulation. The Aces remind us that beginnings are sacred, but they must be nurtured with wisdom. Together, they reveal that the moment we recognize our creative capacity, we also inherit the responsibility to use it consciously. Manifestation becomes both a gift and a moral choice, a reminder that agency and integrity must evolve together.

## Maui Slows the Sun – Polynesian Mythology

The story of Maui begins on a morning when the young demigod feels the world rushing past him. The days are too short — not in theory, but in his bones. He watches fishermen return with half-empty nets, sees his mother squinting in the fading light as she tries to finish her weaving, hears the quiet frustration in the village as darkness steals the hours too quickly.

A heat rises in him, part indignation, part youthful certainty. This isn't how it should be.

And once he feels that truth, he cannot let it go.

Maui does not ask permission from the gods. He does not consult the sun. His conviction is its own force. If the world is out of balance, he will set it right.

He braids a rope from enchanted fibers, each strand humming faintly against his fingertips. His brothers follow him, uneasy but loyal, as he leads them to the place where dawn first touches the earth. The air is cold there, sharp with volcanic stone and the smell of salt. Maui crouches in the half-light, rope coiled in his hands, heart thudding with a mix of fear and exhilaration.

When the sun finally rises, it comes fast — a blazing, living force tearing across the horizon. The heat hits him first, a searing wave that stings his skin. But Maui leaps anyway. He casts the rope, and it catches.

The sun cries out. The ground trembles. Light thrashes around him like a wild animal trying to break free. The rope burns into his palms. His brothers shout in terror.

For a moment, Maui feels the raw power of what he has dared to touch — and a flicker of doubt pierces him. But he holds on. He digs his heels into the earth and pulls with everything he has.

"Slow down," he demands through clenched teeth. "Give us time. Give us life."

The sun strains, furious and brilliant, until its strength falters. Its light dims just enough for Maui to feel the shift — a surrender, or perhaps a negotiation. At last, the sun agrees.

When Maui releases the rope, the world exhales. The sky settles into a new rhythm. His brothers stare at him with awe and something else — a quiet fear of what he has proven himself capable of.

Maui stands triumphant, but the triumph is edged with something he cannot yet name. The air feels different. The balance feels altered. He has changed the world, yes — but he has also tugged at threads he does not fully understand.

This is the Magician in his first form: brilliant, daring, untempered.

The Ace before it becomes a suit.

The spark before it becomes a flame.

Maui's story reminds us that creativity often awakens before wisdom, that action arrives before empathy, and that the power to reshape reality is most dangerous — and most beautiful — when it is still learning how to listen.

## Closing Reflection

The Magician stands at the threshold of power, holding the tools of creation. The Aces mirror his readiness, each offering raw potential in its domain. Together, they remind us that beginnings are powerful, but they are only seeds. Manifestation requires balance, discipline, and integrity.

Modern science tells us that intention alone is never enough; the brain requires repeated action to carve new pathways. In this sense, the Magician is not just a symbol of possibility but of neural commitment — the moment when imagination becomes a pattern the body can follow.

Cosmically, he echoes the early universe: a concentrated point of potential that expands only when directed. Creation is not random; it unfolds through choice, focus, and the willingness to shape raw energy into form.

And in our cultural moment — where distraction is constant and identity is often performed rather than lived — the Magician offers a counter-current. He reminds us that to create is to choose, and every choice shapes the path ahead. His power is not in spectacle but in alignment: the quiet, deliberate act of turning potential into reality.

## Journaling prompt

*What resources or talents do you already have that you could use more consciously right now?*

# The High Priestess and the Twos

## Intuition, Duality, and the Balance of Choice

*"You are what you know, believe, understand, value, trust, inquire of and reveal to yourself."*

*– Excerpt from Tarot Well Done*

## The High Priestess as Number Two: The Mystery Within

The High Priestess sits between two pillars, veiled by symbols of hidden knowledge. She represents the awareness that life is not only material, but also spiritual and subconscious. Her presence reminds us that truth is not always visible, and that wisdom often comes from looking inward rather than outward. She teaches us to hold the tension between knowing and not knowing – the space where intuition begins.

In developmental psychology, this stage reflects the emergence of self-awareness – the realization that there is more beneath the surface than immediate impulses. Spiritually, the High Priestess embodies the divine feminine, intuition, and the mysteries of cycles and polarity. She teaches that opposites – light and dark, conscious and unconscious, masculine and feminine – are not contradictions but complements.

Her lesson is simple yet profound: choices are not only about external outcomes, but about inner alignment. To walk through the veil is to trust that unseen truths are just as real as visible ones.

## The Twos: Choices, Balance, and Duality

The Minor Arcana Twos mirror the High Priestess's archetype. Each Two presents a moment of decision, balance, or partnership. Together, they show how intuition and duality play out in everyday life – through planning, relationships, mental conflict, and material juggling.

### Two of Wands: Planning and Perspective

A man stands on a rooftop, holding a globe and gazing outward. The Two of Wands represents planning, foresight, and the balance between past stability and future possibility. It is the fire of vision – the moment when we realize that our choices shape not only ourselves but the world around us.

Psychologically, this card reflects the stage of broadening perspective – learning to consider contingencies and the needs of others. Spiritually, it reminds us that vision must be tempered by responsibility. The High Priestess's veil is echoed here: we cannot see everything at once, but we must trust our intuition to guide the planning process.

## Two of Cups: Connection and Reciprocity

A man and woman exchange chalices beneath a winged lion. The Two of Cups represents emotional connection, partnership, and the balance of giving and receiving. It is the water of relationship – the moment when two souls recognize each other and choose to unite.

Psychologically, this card reflects the development of intimacy – the ability to form reciprocal bonds that double joy and halve pain. Spiritually, it mirrors the High Priestess's lesson that union is sacred, and that love is both intuitive and practical. The chalices' hourglass shape reminds us that true connection flows both ways.

## Two of Swords: Conflict and Decision

A blindfolded woman sits with crossed swords, protecting her heart. The Two of Swords represents indecision, inner conflict, and the need to balance intellect with intuition. It is the air of thought – the moment when choices feel heavy, and fear clouds clarity.

Psychologically, this card reflects the challenge of decision-making under uncertainty. Spiritually, it echoes the High Priestess's veil: truth may be obscured, but intuition can pierce the blindfold. The lesson is that courage and awareness are needed to move forward, even when outcomes are unclear.

## Two of Pentacles: Juggling and Balance

A young man balances two coins while ships rise and fall on turbulent seas. The Two of Pentacles represents the juggling acts of life — time, money, health, responsibilities. It is the earth of practicality – the moment when we realize that balance is not static, but dynamic.

Psychologically, this card reflects the challenge of managing competing priorities. Spiritually, it reminds us that harmony is not about controlling everything, but about doing what we can and trusting fate with the rest. The High Priestess's wisdom is echoed here: balance is not perfection, but resilience in the face of change.

## The High Priestess and the Twos Together

The High Priestess teaches that life is more than what we see. The Twos show how this truth plays out in daily choices:

- ❖ **Wands (Fire)**: Planning and vision.

- ❖ **Cups (Water)**: Emotional connection and reciprocity.

- ❖ **Swords (Air)**: Mental conflict and decision-making.

- ❖ **Pentacles (Earth)**: Practical juggling and balance.

Every Two asks us to act even when the full picture is not yet visible. Together, they remind us that every choice is both external and internal. Decisions shape outcomes, but they also shape character. The High Priestess's veil is a metaphor for the unseen consequences of our choices, and the Twos are the lived experiences of navigating them.

## Psychological and Spiritual Resonance

From a psychological perspective, the High Priestess and the Twos represent the emergence of discernment – the ability to balance competing forces and trust inner wisdom. They mark the moment when a person begins to sense the difference between impulse and intuition, reaction and reflection. This psychological sensitivity naturally opens into the spiritual dimension, because the ability to discern is inseparable from the recognition that truth often arises from within rather than from external certainty.

From a spiritual perspective, the High Priestess and the Twos embody the principle of duality: that opposites are not enemies, but partners in growth. Where psychology describes the skill of discernment, spirituality describes its purpose – to help us navigate the unseen, the subtle, and the liminal spaces where clarity is still forming.

The High Priestess reminds us that intuition is a valid source of knowledge, especially in the spaces where certainty has not yet taken shape. The Twos remind us that balance is not easy, but it is essential. Together, they reveal that every moment of hesitation, every pause between two possibilities, is a sacred threshold. Choices become invitations to align with truth, and discernment becomes the bridge between the inner world and the outer one.

## Inanna's Descent – Mesopotamian Mythology

The story of Inanna begins with a sensation she cannot name — a tug beneath the ribs, a quiet gravity pulling her toward the Great Below. It is not a command, not a prophecy, not a duty. It is an inner summons, the kind that arrives without explanation and refuses to be ignored.

The realm she approaches belongs to her sister Ereshkigal, a place of shadow, stone, and unfiltered truth. Even from the first gate, the air feels heavier, as though the world itself is holding its breath. Still, Inanna steps forward.

She arrives in full regalia: her crown warm against her brow, her necklace cool on her collarbone, her breastplate gleaming with divine authority. Her ring, her measuring rod, her layered robes — each piece carries the weight of her identity. They are the Mesopotamian echoes of the High Priestess's sacred symbols: the moon, the veil, the scroll, the pillars. They proclaim who she is. But they are not what she is.

At the first gate, the gatekeeper demands her crown. The metal leaves her head with a surprising lightness. At the second, her necklace. The skin beneath it feels suddenly exposed. At the third, her breastplate. She feels the cool air touch her chest.

At each of the seven gates, another symbol falls away — ring, rod, robe — until she stands bare, her divinity no longer displayed but distilled.

She does not resist. She does not bargain. She walks forward, guided only by the quiet pulse of intuition — the High Priestess's deepest teaching: that wisdom is not held in objects, but in the one who carries them.

When Inanna reaches Ereshkigal's throne room, the air is thick with grief and power. Her sister does not greet her. She judges her. She strikes her down. Inanna's body hangs on a hook like a lifeless offering, suspended in a silence so complete it feels like another kind of truth.

Yet even here, something essential is unfolding. In the stillness, Inanna encounters the wisdom that cannot be learned in daylight — the wisdom of shadow, of surrender, of the spaces where identity dissolves and something deeper emerges. She begins to understand the balance between life and death, ascent and descent, knowing and unknowing. She discovers that truth lives not in the garments she once wore, but in the silence beneath them.

After three days, she is revived and allowed to return to the world above. But she does not rise as the goddess who descended. She rises as one who has crossed the threshold between opposites and found that they mirror each other. She rises with a new kind of sight — one that recognizes intuition as truth, and discernment as the fruit of facing what lies beneath the surface.

Inanna's story teaches that inner wisdom is not granted by symbols, titles, or sacred objects. These are expressions of wisdom, not its source. The High Priestess sits among her symbols — the moon, the veil, the scroll — not because she needs them, but because they reflect the knowing she already carries. Like Inanna, she could walk into the underworld naked and still be the High Priestess.

Just like the High Priestess and the Twos, Inanna shows us that intuition is a valid form of knowledge, that duality is sacred, and that every choice is an invitation to align with truth. Her descent reveals that when the symbols fall away, the wisdom remains.

## Closing Reflection

The High Priestess sits between pillars, holding the scroll of wisdom. The Twos mirror her lesson in everyday life – through planning, connection, conflict, and balance. Together, they remind us that choices are not only about outcomes, but about alignment with our deeper selves.

Modern science shows that much of our decision-making happens beneath conscious awareness. Intuition is not an escape from logic but a parallel form of intelligence, shaped by memory, pattern recognition, and the quiet processing that happens when the mind is still. In this way, the High Priestess reflects the hidden architecture of the brain – what we know before we know that we know.

Cosmically, she echoes the dark matter of the universe: unseen, yet shaping everything. Her power is not in visibility but in gravity – the subtle pull toward what is true, even when the path is not illuminated.

And in our cultural moment, where noise often masquerades as clarity and speed is mistaken for certainty, the High Priestess offers a different tempo. She reminds us that intuition is not a luxury – it is a necessity. To trust what lies beyond the veil is to honor the mystery of life, and to walk forward with courage and balance.

## Journaling prompt

*What inner knowing have you been ignoring, and how might you honor it today?*

# The Empress and the Threes

## Fertility, Creativity, and the Abundance of Growth

*"You are a goddess and possess the gift of creation and abundant harvest. You nurture and love, provide security and material comfort. You embody the feminine spirit inherited by the mother, grandmother, and a lengthy line of female ancestry. Life overflows with what you choose to embrace with a generous heart."*

*– Excerpt from Tarot Well Done*

## The Empress as Number Three: The Archetype of Fertility

The Empress is the third card of the Major Arcana, embodying creation, womanhood, and abundance. She sits in a lush paradise, surrounded by forests, rivers, and fields of corn. Her gown of pomegranates connects her to the mysteries of the High

Priestess, but here those mysteries are made manifest in the material world.

She represents the archetype of the mother, the nurturer, and the creative force that brings life into being. Her crown of twelve stars ties her to the cycles of time, while her sceptre points to the heavens, reminding us that creation is both earthly and divine.

Psychologically, the Empress reflects the stage of growth where nurturing and creativity become central. Spiritually, she embodies the principle of abundance: that life flourishes when we embrace generosity, fertility, and care. Her lesson is that growth is not only about survival – it is about thriving, creating, and sharing.

## The Threes: Creativity, Change, and Expansion

The Minor Arcana Threes mirror the Empress's archetype. Each Three represents a moment of creativity, growth, or change. Together, they show how abundance manifests in different domains of life – through enterprise, friendship, pain, and collaboration.

### Three of Wands: Enterprise and Opportunity

A man gazes outward, holding firmly to one wand while leaving two behind. The Three of Wands represents enterprise, ambition, and the courage to embark on new ventures. It is the fire of creativity – the moment when vision becomes action.

Psychologically, this card reflects the stage of taking responsibility for one's growth, learning from past experiences, and bravely facing the unknown. Spiritually, it mirrors the Empress's lesson that abundance comes from courage and commitment. The yellow sky signals awakening, while the three boats remind us that opportunities often expand when we act with intention.

**Three of Cups: Celebration and Community**

Three women raise their chalices in joyful unity, surrounded by flowers and harvest. The Three of Cups represents friendship, community, and the pleasures of shared abundance. It is the water of connection – the moment when joy is multiplied through togetherness.

Psychologically, this card reflects the importance of social bonds and the emotional nourishment of belonging. Spiritually, it echoes the Empress's nurturing energy, showing that abundance is not only material but relational. The diverse robes of the women remind us that collective success comes from valuing different contributions.

**Three of Swords: Pain and Growth**

A heart pierced by three swords hangs in a stormy sky. The Three of Swords represents pain, miscommunication, and emotional wounds. It is the air of intellect – the moment when clarity cuts deeply but also teaches.

Psychologically, this card reflects the reality that growth often comes through hardship. Spiritually, it mirrors the Empress's fertility in a paradoxical way: even wounds can become teachers. The oversized heart reminds us that pain, though real, can be endured and transformed. The lesson is that abundance is not only joy – it is resilience born from suffering.

**Three of Pentacles: Collaboration and Craft**

Three figures convene at the entrance of a cathedral, each contributing their unique role. The Three of Pentacles represents teamwork, collaboration, and the pooling of resources for a higher purpose. It is the earth of practicality – the moment when creativity becomes structure.

Psychologically, this card reflects the importance of cooperation and the recognition that growth often requires collective effort. Spiritually, it echoes the Empress's abundance, showing that creation is not solitary but communal. The stonemason's elevated position reminds us that skill and craftsmanship are vital, while the blackened coins hint at the complexity of human motives.

# The Empress and the Threes Together

The Empress teaches that abundance is the natural outcome of nurturing and creativity. The Threes show how this abundance manifests in daily life:

- **Wands (Fire)**: Enterprise and opportunity.

- **Cups (Water)**: Celebration and community.

- **Swords (Air)**: Pain and growth through clarity.

- **Pentacles (Earth)**: Collaboration and craftsmanship.

Together, they remind us that growth is multifaceted. It can be joyful, painful, communal, or courageous. Growth rarely looks the same from one moment to the next. The Empress's lesson is that all forms of growth – whether through joy or hardship – are part of the fertile cycle of life.

# Psychological and Spiritual Resonance

From a psychological perspective, the Empress and the Threes represent the stage of creativity and expansion – where nurturing energy leads to growth. They reflect the moment when inner resources begin to express themselves outwardly, when care becomes creation and potential becomes form. This psychological movement toward expansion naturally opens into the spiritual dimension, because the impulse to create is inseparable from the deeper truth that life itself seeks expression through us.

From a spiritual perspective, the Empress and the Threes embody the principle of abundance: that life flourishes when we embrace both joy and pain, both individuality and community. Where psychology describes how growth unfolds, spirituality describes why it matters – revealing that abundance is not merely a result of effort, but a reflection of alignment with the generative forces of life.

The Empress reminds us that creation is sacred. The Threes remind us that growth is a natural impulse – even if it unfolds unevenly – and takes many forms. Together, they reveal that abundance is not measured by outcome alone, but by the richness of experience that emerges when we allow life to move through us. Creativity becomes a dialogue with the world, and expansion becomes a sign that we are participating in something larger than ourselves.

## Demeter and Persephone – Greek Mythology

The story of Demeter begins in a world overflowing with life. As the goddess of grain, growth, and nourishment, she moves through the fields like sunlight made flesh. Wherever her hands pass, wheat rises. Wherever her breath falls, orchards swell with fruit. The earth responds to her the way a child responds to a mother's touch — with trust, with abundance, with effortless flourishing.

In these early days, Demeter is the Empress in her purest form: creation as devotion, nurturing as power, life as something she pours from herself into the world.

One afternoon, her daughter Persephone wanders into a meadow, drawn by wildflowers shimmering in the heat. The air is bright, the grass soft, the world unthreatening. And then — a rupture. The ground opens, Hades emerges, and Persephone is taken into the underworld before anyone can cry out.

When Demeter discovers her daughter's absence, the world that once bloomed under her touch begins to recoil. She searches the earth with frantic footsteps, calling Persephone's name until her voice breaks. Her grief is not quiet. It is a force. She refuses to tend the fields, refuses to coax life from the soil, refuses to let the world be beautiful while her daughter is gone.

The earth mirrors her sorrow. Wheat shrivels. Fruit drops unripe from the trees. The air grows thin and cold. Humanity feels the hunger of a goddess undone.

Demeter's grief becomes part of the world's heartbeat — a reminder that abundance is never separate from loss, that creation and heartbreak are woven from the same threads.

Eventually, a compromise is forged: Persephone will spend part of the year in the underworld and part of the year with her mother. When Persephone rises, Demeter's joy returns like spring wind, and the earth blossoms in relief. When Persephone descends, Demeter mourns again, and the world grows quiet, the soil folding into itself.

Through this cycle, Demeter learns that creation is not a single act but a continual unfolding — growth, loss, renewal, return. She learns that nurturing energy is powerful, but it cannot shield her from pain. And she learns that love, when it meets loss, does not disappear; it transforms into cycles, seasons, and stories.

The Empress teaches that creation is sacred, and the Threes teach that growth takes many forms — birth, expansion, contraction, renewal. Demeter embodies this truth. She shows us that abundance is not only the harvest we gather, but the fullness of experience: joy and sorrow, presence and absence, individuality and connection.

Just like the Empress and the Threes, Demeter reminds us that life flourishes when we nurture what we love, honor what we lose, and trust that every season — even the barren ones — is part of the greater cycle of becoming.

## Closing Reflection

The Empress sits in her paradise, embodying fertility and abundance. The Threes mirror her lesson in everyday life —

through enterprise, celebration, pain, and collaboration. Together, they remind us that growth is not linear, but cyclical.

Biology reminds us that all living systems grow through cycles: expansion, rest, repair, and renewal. Even creativity follows this pattern, with bursts of inspiration followed by quieter phases where ideas take root beneath the surface. The Empress reflects this natural intelligence — the way life unfolds when it is given space to breathe.

Cosmically, she echoes the generative forces of the universe itself. Stars are born from collapse and expansion, galaxies form through interaction, and nothing grows in isolation. Her abundance is not excess; it is the steady pulse of creation woven into the fabric of existence.

And in our cultural moment, where productivity is often mistaken for worth and constant output is celebrated, the Empress offers a gentler truth. Abundance often begins with what we choose to nurture. To embrace creativity, to value connection, to learn from pain, and to collaborate with others is to live in the fullness of life — not through striving, but through participation in the cycles that sustain us.

## Journaling prompt

*Where can you nurture growth – within yourself, your relationships, or your creative projects?*

# The Emperor and the Fours

## Structure, Stability, the Anchors of Life

*"You are a pioneer in the world, unafraid to stake your claim and cultivate your environment. Your power is tempered by your ability to self-regulate your ego. You create order and follow your ambition with vigour and without fear. You embody the male spirit inherited by the father, grandfather, and a lengthy line of male ancestry. You explore new possibilities and remain undaunted. Despite the desert, you will grow a garden to harvest for those who rely on your protection and the security you provide."*

*– Excerpt from Tarot Well Done*

### The Emperor as Number Four: The Archetype of Structure

The Emperor sits upright on his stone throne, alert and commanding. He represents the archetypal father – authority, rules, and protection. His presence is reassuring when upright, but can become restrictive when reversed. Where the Empress nurtures through abundance, the Emperor stabilizes through order.

Psychologically, the Emperor reflects the developmental stage of learning boundaries and discipline. Spiritually, he embodies the principle of structure: that growth requires foundations, and freedom requires responsibility. His lesson is that power must be tempered by self-regulation, and that true authority is protective, not domineering.

## The Fours: Anchors, Stability, and Foundations

The Minor Arcana Fours mirror the Emperor's archetype. Each Four represents a form of stability – whether in community, emotion, thought, or material security. Together, they show how structure anchors us in different domains of life.

### Four of Wands: Community and Celebration

A couple rejoices beneath a garland strung between four wands, with a castle and community behind them. The Four of Wands represents celebration, belonging, and the safety of group achievements. It is the fire of stability – the moment when joy is anchored in community.

Psychologically, this card reflects the importance of social structures – family, friendships, and society – as sources of protection and meaning. Spiritually, it echoes the Emperor's lesson that stability is not only personal, but collective. The gateway of wands invites us to step into shared joy and security.

## Four of Cups: Contemplation and Self-Protection

A man sits beneath a tree, arms crossed, contemplating a chalice offered by a cloud. The Four of Cups represents introspection, mindfulness, and the need to pause before acting on impulse. It is the water of stability – the moment when emotions are anchored through reflection.

Psychologically, this card reflects the importance of pausing to consider consequences, rather than rushing into decisions. Spiritually, it mirrors the Emperor's discipline, showing that emotional stability requires boundaries and self-awareness. The lesson is that true security comes from listening to both heart and mind.

## Four of Swords: Rest and Withdrawal

A knight lies upon a tomb in a chapel, hands folded in prayer, with swords suspended above him. The Four of Swords represents rest, withdrawal, and the need to regain perspective. It is the air of stability – the moment when thought is anchored through pause.

Psychologically, this card reflects the necessity of rest and recovery, especially after conflict or stress. Spiritually, it echoes the Emperor's protective authority, reminding us that discipline includes knowing when to stop. The stained-glass window suggests that perception can be renewed when we allow ourselves time to regroup.

## Four of Pentacles: Material Security and Possession

A man sits on a stone bench, clutching a coin to his chest, with others beneath his feet and atop his crown. The Four of Pentacles represents material security, stability, and the desire to protect possessions. It is the earth of stability – the moment when wellbeing is anchored through resources.

Psychologically, this card reflects the importance of financial and material foundations, but also the risk of over-attachment. Spiritually, it mirrors the Emperor's authority, showing that security can be protective or restrictive. The lesson is that material stability is valuable, but must not dominate our identity.

## The Emperor and the Fours Together

The Emperor teaches that structure and discipline create stability. Stability is not the absence of change, but the structure that helps us navigate it. The Fours show this stability manifesting in daily life:

- ❖ **Wands (Fire)**: Community and shared celebration.

- ❖ **Cups (Water)**: Emotional introspection and self-protection.

- ❖ **Swords (Air)**: Rest and mental clarity through withdrawal.

- ❖ **Pentacles (Earth)**: Material security and possession.

Together, they remind us that stability is multifaceted. It can be joyful, reflective, restful, or protective. The Emperor's lesson is that true authority creates anchors, not chains.

## Psychological and Spiritual Resonance

From a psychological perspective, the Emperor and the Fours represent the stage of establishing boundaries, discipline, and foundations. They reflect the moment when structure becomes a form of self-support rather than self-restriction. This psychological grounding naturally opens into the spiritual dimension, because the need for stability is inseparable from the deeper truth that growth requires a place to root.

From a spiritual perspective, the Emperor and the Fours embody the principle of anchoring: that growth requires stability, and that security allows us to flourish. Where psychology describes how foundations are built, spirituality describes why they matter – revealing that structure is not an obstacle to freedom, but the soil in which freedom can take shape.

The Emperor reminds us that authority must be tempered by responsibility. The Fours remind us that stability takes many forms. Together, they reveal that structure is not about rigidity, but about creating the conditions in which life can expand with confidence. Foundations become acts of care, and discipline becomes a way of honoring what we are capable of becoming.

## Marduk's Story – Babylonian Mythology

The story of Marduk begins in a world on the brink of collapse. The younger gods have stirred the primordial waters, and from their disturbance rises Tiamat — the great dragon of chaos, older than memory, vast as the sea itself. Storms coil around her. Monsters gather in her wake. The air thickens with the taste of salt and lightning. The cosmos trembles as if its bones are loosening.

No god is strong enough to face her. Order dissolves. Stability slips like sand through open hands. Then Marduk steps forward.

He is young, but his power is unmistakable — a sharp, rising force, like a mountain forming beneath the ocean. He sees clearly what the others cannot: that if no one acts, the world will unravel. He offers to confront Tiamat, not for glory, but to protect creation itself. The gods, desperate and afraid, grant him authority for the task. Their voices echo like wind through hollow stone.

Armed with wind, net, and bow, Marduk enters the storm. The air around him roars. His net hums with divine tension. His bowstring thrums against his fingertips. When he faces Tiamat, she rises like a living horizon — scales shimmering, jaws wide enough to swallow the sky.

The battle shakes the cosmos. Winds scream. Waters convulse. Light fractures. But Marduk holds his ground. With precision and force, he binds her, pierces her, and brings an end to the chaos that threatened creation.

From her vast body, he shapes the world. The sky from her ribs. The mountains from her spine. The rivers from her eyes.

He sets the stars in their courses, establishes the seasons, and writes the first laws into the fabric of existence. Through his strength and order, life becomes possible. Marduk embodies the Emperor's gift — the ability to build from almost nothing, to create stability where there was once only uncertainty.

But as Marduk's authority grows, so does the temptation to control. The gods, grateful for his protection, elevate him as king of the cosmos. His word becomes law. His order becomes increasingly hierarchical. What began as protective strength begins to calcify. The structure he created starts to harden. The balance he restored begins to tilt.

Marduk feels the shift — the subtle pleasure of being obeyed, the tightening grip of certainty, the creeping belief that order must be maintained at any cost. He must learn that authority without self-regulation becomes tyranny, and that order without compassion becomes oppression.

Marduk's story teaches that the Emperor's power is sacred when it protects, but dangerous when it seeks to dominate. Stability requires strength, but also restraint. Authority requires clarity, but also humility. The Fours remind us that growth needs structure; the Emperor reminds us that structure must remain flexible enough to serve life, not stifle it.

Just like the Emperor and the Fours, Marduk shows us that true authority is not domination, but stewardship — the ability to create order without extinguishing the freedom and vitality it is meant to protect.

## Closing Reflection

The Emperor sits on his throne, embodying authority and discipline. The Fours mirror his lesson in everyday life — through community, contemplation, rest, and material security. Together, they remind us that stability is the anchor of growth.

In nature, structure is not rigidity but support. Ecosystems thrive because of boundaries: roots hold the soil, bones hold the body, and even the mind relies on predictable patterns to reduce cognitive strain. The Emperor reflects this biological truth — that form creates freedom, and stability allows energy to flow where it is needed most.

Cosmically, he echoes the forces that hold the universe together. Gravity shapes galaxies, orbits create order, and nothing can grow without a center of mass to anchor it. His authority is not domination but coherence — the quiet strength that keeps a system from collapsing into chaos.

And in our cultural moment, where authority is often mistrusted and structure is sometimes seen as constraint, the Emperor offers a different perspective. True power protects rather than oppresses. To embrace structure, to value stability, and to build secure foundations is to live with strength and resilience — not as an act of control, but as an act of care.

## Journaling prompt

*What structures or boundaries in your life support you, and which ones restrict you?*

# The Hierophant and the Fives

## Tradition, Instability, and the Testing of Systems

*"You possess the key to proclaim what is sacred. To unlock the door, you must first accept with an open heart and settle yourself within a pattern of recognisable truths."*

*– Excerpt from Tarot Well Done*

## The Hierophant as Number Five: The Archetype of Tradition

The Hierophant sits between pillars, blessing acolytes, holding the keys to sacred knowledge. He represents tradition, systems, and the frameworks that provide meaning and stability. Where the Emperor established secular order, the Hierophant introduces spiritual and societal order. His lesson is that belonging to a system – whether religious, cultural, or communal – can provide safety and identity, but also risks dogma, rigidity, and exclusion.

Psychologically, the Hierophant reflects the stage of learning from established structures – schools, religions, governments, families. Spiritually, he embodies the principle of tradition: that wisdom is passed down but must be interpreted with discernment. His presence reminds us that systems can anchor us, but they must not enslave us. Tradition can be an anchor that steadies us, but it can also become an obstacle when it resists necessary change.

# The Fives: Instability, Conflict, and Testing of Systems

The Minor Arcana Fives mirror the Hierophant's archetype. Each Five represents instability, conflict, or challenge – the moments when systems are tested, and when belonging or meaning is questioned. Together, they show how tradition and structure can both support and constrain.

## Five of Wands: Conflict and Competition

Five youths clash with wands, each pursuing their own ego-driven desires. The Five of Wands represents arguments, tension, and competition. It is the fire of instability – the moment when collective energy fractures into individual pursuits.

Psychologically, this card reflects the challenge of learning to cooperate within systems, rather than fighting for dominance. Spiritually, it mirrors the Hierophant's lesson that systems require cohesion, and that ego disrupts harmony. The mimic warfare reminds us that not all battles are real, but even performative conflict drains energy.

## Five of Cups: Loss and Emotional Exhaustion

A cloaked figure mourns spilled cups, blind to the two still upright. The Five of Cups represents grief, regret, and emotional defeat. It is the water of instability – the moment when emotional connection to systems feels broken.

Psychologically, this card reflects the pain of loss, whether personal or communal. Spiritually, it mirrors the Hierophant's lesson that systems can fail us, but healing comes through reconnection. The bridge and upright cups remind us that support is available, if we lift our gaze beyond despair.

## Five of Swords: Ruthless Victory and Broken Trust

A victor gloats while others retreat, swords discarded. The Five of Swords represents conflict, bullying, and victory at the expense of others. It is the air of instability – the moment when intellect is used to dominate rather than to connect.

Psychologically, this card reflects the danger of winning without integrity. Spiritually, it mirrors the Hierophant's lesson that systems can be manipulated, and that justice is not always served. The grey clouds remind us that conflict often arises from bruised egos and misconceptions, not truth.

**Five of Pentacles: Hardship and Exclusion**

Two impoverished figures pass a church window, alone in the snow. The Five of Pentacles represents poverty, illness, and exclusion. It is the earth of instability – the moment when material systems fail to provide support.

Psychologically, this card reflects the pain of abandonment and inequality. Spiritually, it mirrors the Hierophant's lesson that faith must be lived, not performed. The inverted pentacle in the stained-glass window warns of false faith – systems that claim virtue but deny compassion. The lesson is that true tradition must embody care and inclusion.

# The Hierophant and the Fives Together

The Hierophant teaches that systems provide meaning and safety. The Fives show how those systems are tested:

- ❖ **Wands (Fire)**: Conflict and competition within groups.

- ❖ **Cups (Water)**: Emotional loss and the need for reconnection.

- ❖ **Swords (Air)**: Ruthless victory and manipulation of truth.

- ❖ **Pentacles (Earth)**: Material hardship and exclusion.

Together, they remind us that tradition and systems are not perfect. They can anchor us, but they can also fracture, exclude, or oppress. Tradition can steady us, but it can also resist the very growth it once protected. The Hierophant's lesson is that systems must be lived with integrity, and that instability is part of growth.


## Psychological and Spiritual Resonance

From a psychological perspective, the Hierophant and the Fives represent the stage of testing boundaries – learning how systems support us, and how they fail. They reflect the moment when a person begins to question inherited structures and evaluate which traditions still serve growth. This psychological questioning naturally opens into the spiritual dimension, because the need to understand systems is inseparable from the deeper search for meaning within them.

From a spiritual perspective, the Hierophant and the Fives embody the principle of discernment: that tradition must be interpreted with compassion, and that instability is a call to growth. Where psychology describes how systems are tested, spirituality describes why those tests matter – revealing that disruption is often the doorway through which deeper wisdom emerges.

The Hierophant reminds us that belonging is sacred. The Fives remind us that belonging can feel fragile. Together, they reveal that systems must evolve if they are to remain alive, and that conflict and loss are invitations to refine what we hold sacred. Instability becomes a teacher, and questioning becomes a path toward more authentic connection.

## Chiron's Wound – Greek Mythology

The story of Chiron begins at the edge of two worlds. Born a centaur, he carries the body of a creature known for wildness and excess, yet his spirit is gentle, disciplined, and wise. From an early age, he turns toward study — medicine, music, prophecy, the sacred arts. His mind is as steady as his heartbeat. Over time, gods and heroes travel to him for guidance, drawn by the calm clarity in his presence.

Chiron becomes a bridge between instinct and insight, chaos and order, the human and the divine. He embodies the

Hierophant's gift: the ability to transmit wisdom across generations.

On Mount Pelion, he builds a school among the pines. The air there is sharp with resin and mountain wind. Young heroes gather at his hearth, where he teaches not only archery and healing, but ethics — how to use power with responsibility, how to honor tradition without becoming bound by it. His lessons create a sense of belonging, a lineage of knowledge that shapes the future of Greece.

Yet even as he upholds tradition, Chiron knows that systems must evolve. He teaches each student differently, adjusting the old ways to meet new needs. His authority is rooted not in rigidity, but in compassion — a living tradition rather than a fixed one.

One day, during a gathering of heroes, a poisoned arrow is loosed by accident. It whistles through the air and strikes Chiron in the thigh. The moment is quiet at first — a stunned breath, a widening of eyes — and then the pain arrives, sharp and unrelenting. Though immortal, he cannot heal the wound. The poison burns through him without mercy.

The system he upheld — the world of heroes, weapons, and divine order — has failed him. His belonging is revealed to be fragile. His role as teacher does not shield him from suffering. This is the Five: the rupture that exposes the limits of tradition, the moment when the structure cracks and reveals its imperfections.

Chiron does not retreat into bitterness. Instead, he turns inward, seeking meaning within the wound. He realizes that wisdom is not only passed down through teachings, but also through the experiences that break us open. His pain becomes a teacher, too — one that speaks in a language older than words.

In an act of profound discernment, he offers to give up his immortality so that Prometheus may be freed from his punishment. Through this sacrifice, Chiron transforms his suffering into service, reshaping the very structure of divine justice. His wound becomes a doorway through which new wisdom enters the world.

Chiron's story teaches that systems, no matter how sacred, are imperfect. Belonging is precious, but it is not guaranteed. Tradition offers guidance, but it must be interpreted with compassion and adapted to the needs of the present.

The Fives remind us that instability is not a failure — it is an invitation to deepen meaning. The Hierophant reminds us that wisdom is not static; it evolves through the very challenges that test it.

Just like the Hierophant and the Fives, Chiron shows us that true teaching comes from humility, that belonging must be tended with care, and that the wounds we receive from our systems can become the very places where new wisdom is born.

## Closing Reflection

The Hierophant sits as a representative of tradition, blessing those who seek meaning. The Fives mirror his lesson in everyday life – through conflict, grief, ruthless victory, and exclusion. Together, they remind us that systems are both anchors and tests.

In human behaviour, we see that rituals and shared structures reduce cognitive load, helping the mind navigate uncertainty. Yet the same systems can become rigid when they are no longer questioned. The Hierophant reflects this dual nature — the way our brains seek order, even as growth requires us to revise the patterns we inherit.

Cosmically, he echoes the tension between order and entropy. The universe itself is shaped by forces that build structure and forces that break it down, and meaning emerges in the interplay between the two. Tradition, like matter, must continually reorganise to stay alive.

And in our cultural moment — where institutions are both challenged and defended with equal fervour — the Hierophant offers a steadying reminder. Tradition is not static; it must be lived, questioned, and renewed. To embrace systems with integrity, to face instability with courage, and to seek meaning beyond dogma is to walk the path of growth.

## Journaling prompt

*What traditions or systems shape your choices, and do they still serve your growth?*

# The Lovers and the Sixes

## Union, Harmony, and the Choices of Connection

*"Your paradise union exists within the sun, and the soul who matches yours will know of practicality as the way toward blissful union. It is most practical to learn to know yourself first and to place expectations on another to know you second."*

*– Excerpt from Tarot Well Done*

### The Lovers as Number Six: The Archetype of Union

The Lovers is the sixth card of the Major Arcana, depicting the first true union of male and female principles. It represents choice, relationship, and the turning points that arise when we decide to join our path with another. The Lovers remind us that relationships are not only about passion – they are about decisions that shape destiny. Their deeper teaching is that choice is a form of alignment – a way of bringing our actions into harmony with our values, desires, and truth.

Psychologically, the Lovers reflect the developmental stage of intimacy and partnership – the realization that our choices affect not only ourselves but those we unite with. Spiritually, they embody the principle of integration: that wholeness comes from balancing opposites, and that love is both practical and transcendent. Their lesson is that union requires self-knowledge, honesty, and discernment.

## The Sixes: Harmony, Reciprocity, and Communication

The Minor Arcana Sixes mirror the Lovers' archetype. Each Six represents harmony, reciprocity, and the communication that sustains relationships. Together, they show how union and choice play out in everyday life – through victory, nostalgia, transition, and generosity.

### Six of Wands: Victory and Recognition

A horseman rides in triumph, laurel wreath raised, surrounded by admirers. The Six of Wands represents victory, achievement, and public recognition. It is the fire of harmony – the moment when individual success is acknowledged by the collective.

Psychologically, this card reflects the importance of validation and encouragement in relationships and communities. Spiritually, it mirrors the Lovers' lesson that union requires communication and recognition. Success is sweeter when shared, but recognition is best held with humility.

## Six of Cups: Nostalgia and Innocence

Two figures exchange a chalice of flowers in a village square. The Six of Cups represents nostalgia, childhood memories, and the sweetness of past connections. It is the water of harmony – the moment when emotional bonds are remembered and cherished.

Psychologically, this card reflects the role of memory in shaping identity and relationships. Spiritually, it mirrors the Lovers' lesson that union is not only about the present – it is also about the stories we carry from the past. The challenge is to honor memory without letting it overshadow the present.

## Six of Swords: Transition and Recovery

A ferryman carries passengers across calm waters toward a serene landscape. The Six of Swords represents transition, recovery, and moving on from turbulence. It is the air of harmony – the moment when clarity and communication guide us toward peace.

Psychologically, this card reflects the importance of leaving behind conflict and embracing new perspectives. Spiritually, it mirrors the Lovers' lesson that union sometimes requires departure – from old patterns, toxic relationships, or limiting beliefs. Harmony is found in the courage to move forward.

**Six of Pentacles: Generosity and Reciprocity**

A nobleman distributes coins to beggars, scales in hand. The Six of Pentacles represents generosity, charity, and the balance of giving and receiving. It is the earth of harmony – the moment when material abundance is shared.

Psychologically, this card reflects the importance of reciprocity in relationships – support must flow both ways. Spiritually, it mirrors the Lovers' lesson that union requires fairness and integrity. True generosity is not about status – it is about genuine care and balance.

## The Lovers and the Sixes Together

The Lovers teach that union and choice shape destiny. The Sixes show how harmony manifests in daily life:

- **Wands (Fire)**: Victory and recognition.

- **Cups (Water)**: Nostalgia and emotional bonds.

- **Swords (Air)**: Transition and recovery.

- **Pentacles (Earth)**: Generosity and reciprocity.

Together, they remind us that relationships are sustained by communication, fairness, and shared meaning. The Lovers' lesson is that union is not only about passion – it is about the choices that create harmony. Harmony is sustained when our choices align with our values, not just our desires.

## Psychological and Spiritual Resonance

From a psychological perspective, the Lovers and the Sixes represent the stage of integration – learning to balance individuality with partnership, and past with present. They reflect the moment when a person begins to understand that identity is shaped not only internally but also in relationship. This psychological movement toward integration naturally opens into the spiritual dimension, because the work of balancing self and other is inseparable from the deeper truth that connection is a sacred act.

From a spiritual perspective, the Lovers and the Sixes embody the principle of harmony: that love and union are sustained by reciprocity, communication, and fairness. Where psychology describes how integration unfolds, spirituality describes what it is for – revealing that harmony is not merely emotional ease, but a conscious alignment with the relational forces that shape human experience.

The Lovers remind us that choices in relationships are sacred because they reveal what we are aligned with. The Sixes remind us that harmony is practical, lived daily in recognition, memory, transition, and generosity. Together, they reveal that union is both a gift and a responsibility – an ongoing practice of choosing alignment, tending to connection, and allowing relationship to become a site of mutual growth.

## Izanagi and Izanami – Japanese Shinto Mythology

The story of Izanagi and Izanami begins at the edge of creation, when the world is still a swirling sea of mist. The air is cool and formless, the horizon undefined. The elder gods place a jeweled spear in their hands — its surface glimmering with the first hints of light — and ask them to bring shape to the unshaped.

Standing together on the Floating Bridge of Heaven, they lean over the vastness below. When they stir the waters, the sound is soft but immense, like the first breath of the world. As they lift the spear, droplets fall and solidify into the first island. Their union becomes the source of creation — a partnership rooted in reciprocity, intention, and shared purpose. They embody the Lovers' teaching that union is not merely emotional; it is generative.

Izanagi and Izanami descend to the new land and build a pillar around which they perform a sacred marriage ritual. The air is warm, the earth still young beneath their feet. But their first attempt falters. Izanami speaks first, and the child they create is malformed. Confused and sorrowful, they seek guidance. The gods explain that harmony requires balance — each partner must honor the other's voice, each must participate in the ritual with fairness and respect.

When they repeat the ceremony with mutual recognition, their union becomes fruitful. Islands rise from the sea. Mountains push upward. Rivers carve their paths. Deities emerge like sparks from a shared flame. This is the Sixes' reminder that harmony is practical, lived through communication, ritual, and daily acts of balance.

But creation is not without cost. When Izanami gives birth to the fire god, the heat sears her body. She cries out, and the world trembles. She dies in agony, and the land they built together falls silent. Izanagi is undone. The harmony they sustained dissolves into grief. This is the moment of the Sixes' shadow — the transition from presence to absence, from union to memory.

Unable to accept the loss, Izanagi journeys to Yomi, the land of the dead. The air grows heavy as he descends. The light fades. The world narrows into darkness.

In that darkness, he calls out to Izanami. Her voice answers — faint, distant, familiar. She tells him she has eaten the food of the underworld and cannot return, yet she asks him to trust her and wait while she petitions the rulers of Yomi for release. Izanagi agrees, but fear coils in his chest. The silence stretches. The uncertainty becomes unbearable.

He lights a torch.

In that moment, he sees her decaying form — a body returning to shadow. Izanami, shamed and enraged by his breach of trust, rises in fury. She chases him from the underworld, her footsteps echoing like thunder. Their bond shatters. The Lovers' teaching becomes clear: choices in relationships are sacred, and the desire for truth must be balanced with respect for boundaries.

When Izanagi escapes to the world above, he collapses beside a river and performs a ritual of purification. As he washes away the darkness of Yomi, droplets fall from his skin and become new deities — including Amaterasu, the sun goddess. Even in separation, their union continues to create. Memory becomes transition. Loss becomes renewal. This is the Sixes' deepest wisdom: harmony is not static; it evolves through movement, generosity, and the willingness to begin again.

Izanagi and Izanami's story teaches that love is both a gift and a responsibility. Their union creates the world, but their choices shape its rhythms — day and night, life and death, presence and absence. The Lovers remind us that partnership requires conscious choice and mutual respect. The Sixes remind us that harmony is sustained through communication, fairness, and the courage to navigate transition. Their myth reveals that integration is not the absence of conflict, but the willingness to meet each other — and ourselves — with honesty, reciprocity, and care.

Just like the Lovers and the Sixes, Izanagi and Izanami show us that union is sacred, fragile, and transformative. It asks us to balance individuality with partnership, past with present, and desire with discernment — creating a harmony that is lived, not assumed.

## Closing Reflection

The Lovers stand beneath the sun, blessed by an angel, embodying union and choice. The Sixes mirror their lesson in everyday life – through victory, nostalgia, recovery, and generosity. Together, they remind us that harmony is not accidental – it is chosen, nurtured, and sustained.

Neuroscience shows that connection is not merely emotional but physiological; the body attunes to those we trust, synchronizing breath, heartbeat, and even neural rhythms. In this way, the Lovers reflect a biological truth — that union is not just a feeling but a pattern the nervous system learns to share.

Cosmically, they echo the dance of celestial bodies: two forces moving in relation, each influencing the other's path. Harmony

emerges not from sameness but from gravitational balance —
the steady exchange that keeps an orbit intact.

And in our cultural moment, where relationships are often
idealised or commodified, the Lovers offer a more grounded
wisdom. True union requires self-knowledge, fairness, and
communication. To embrace love, to honor memory, to move
forward, and to give generously is to live in harmony — not as a
fantasy, but as a daily practice of choosing one another and
choosing oneself.

## Journaling prompt

*What important choice or relationship in your life is asking for
deeper alignment with your values?*

# The Chariot and the Sevens

## Willpower, Tests, and the Path of Perseverance

*"Your courage to face truth, respect difference and reach compromise, sets your guiding path towards shared victory with others."*

*– Excerpt from Tarot Well Done*

## The Chariot as Number Seven: The Archetype of Willpower

The Chariot is the seventh card of the Major Arcana, representing the culmination of lessons learned so far in the Fool's journey. It embodies willpower, direction, and mastery – the ability to harness opposing forces and move forward with determination. The Chariot reminds us that progress is not accidental; it is the result of conscious choice, negotiation, and respect for diversity. Its deeper teaching is that willpower is not just about movement, but about choosing direction over distraction – guiding energy rather than scattering it.

Psychologically, the Chariot reflects the stage of developing autonomy and self-control – the realization that success requires discipline and compromise. Spiritually, it embodies the principle of mastery: that true victory comes not from domination, but from guiding diverse forces toward a shared path. Its lesson is that perseverance and respect for difference lead to progress.

## The Sevens: Tests, Challenges, and Perseverance

The Minor Arcana Sevens mirror the Chariot's archetype. Each Seven represents a test, a challenge, or a prolonged effort – the moments when willpower is stretched and perseverance is required. Together, they show how determination manifests in creativity, emotion, intellect, and material pursuits.

### Seven of Wands: Courage and Standing Ground

A man stands disproportionately large against the landscape, holding a wand against six others. The Seven of Wands represents courage, challenge, and prolonged effort. It is the fire of perseverance – the moment when we must stand our ground and prove our purpose.

Psychologically, this card reflects the challenge of defending one's position against opposition. Spiritually, it mirrors the Chariot's lesson that mastery requires confidence and resilience. The mismatched shoes remind us that confidence alone does not prove purpose – integrity and fairness must accompany determination.

## Seven of Cups: Fantasy and Choices

A dark figure orchestrates cups filled with illusions, floating on clouds. The Seven of Cups represents fantasy, imagination, and the confusion of too many choices. It is the water of perseverance – the moment when emotional clarity is tested by illusion.

Psychologically, this card reflects the challenge of discerning reality from fantasy, and of making choices that serve rather than enslave us. Spiritually, it mirrors the Chariot's lesson that direction requires clarity – without it, willpower is wasted on illusions. The test is to choose wisely, and to trust intuition over deception.

## Seven of Swords: Entitlement and Responsibility

A man tiptoes from a campsite, carrying swords, looking back at what remains. The Seven of Swords represents stealth, strategy, and responsibility. It is the air of perseverance – the moment when intellect is tested by choices of integrity.

Psychologically, this card reflects the challenge of balancing responsibility with entitlement – whether reclaiming what is ours or succumbing to deceit. Spiritually, it mirrors the Chariot's lesson that mastery requires honesty. The test is whether we act with integrity or allow cunning to undermine trust.

**Seven of Pentacles: Discontent and Patience**

A weary man leans on his hoe, gazing at a barren vine of pentacles. The Seven of Pentacles represents disappointment, missed opportunities, and the need for patience. It is the earth of perseverance – the moment when material effort is tested by delay or failure.

Psychologically, this card reflects the challenge of coping with discontent and deciding whether to persist or redirect effort. Spiritually, it mirrors the Chariot's lesson that mastery requires patience and adaptability. The test is whether we learn from disappointment and adjust our path or continue investing in what no longer bears fruit.

## The Chariot and the Sevens Together

The Chariot teaches that willpower and mastery guide progress. The Sevens show how perseverance is tested in daily life:

- ❖ **Wands (Fire)**: Courage and standing ground.

- ❖ **Cups (Water)**: Fantasy and discerning choices.

- ❖ **Swords (Air)**: Responsibility and integrity.

- ❖ **Pentacles (Earth)**: Discontent and patience.

Together, they remind us that progress requires resilience, clarity, honesty, and adaptability. Perseverance is not only about effort – it is about directing effort toward what truly matters. The Chariot's lesson is that true mastery is not about avoiding tests – it is about facing them with courage and wisdom.


## Psychological and Spiritual Resonance

From a psychological perspective, the Chariot and the Sevens represent the stage of perseverance – learning to face challenges, defend positions, and adapt to disappointment. They reflect the moment when a person begins to understand that resilience is not only a reaction to adversity but a skill that develops through repeated testing. This psychological strengthening naturally opens into the spiritual dimension, because the work of perseverance is inseparable from the deeper truth that mastery is an inner alignment, not an outer conquest.

From a spiritual perspective, the Chariot and the Sevens embody the principle of mastery: that victory is not about domination, but about guiding diverse forces toward harmony. Where psychology describes how perseverance forms, spirituality describes what it is for — revealing that mastery is not the absence of struggle, but the ability to remain centered while navigating it.

The Chariot reminds us that willpower is sacred. The Sevens remind us that perseverance is essential. Together, they reveal that mastery is shaped through the tests we face, and that every challenge is an invitation to refine our direction, deepen our resolve, and align our actions with purpose.

## Arjuna's Dilemma — Hindu Tradition

Arjuna's story unfolds on a vast battlefield at dawn, where two armies gather beneath a sky heavy with dust and anticipation. The air vibrates with the clang of armor, the snort of war-horses, the murmured prayers of soldiers preparing to face their own destinies. Each army carries a different vision of justice, loyalty, and fate — and Arjuna, a warrior of unmatched skill, rides into the center of it all.

His chariot is drawn by two horses: one restless, pawing at the earth, eager to surge forward; the other steady, breathing slow and deep. Their opposing rhythms mirror the conflict rising within him. The Chariot's teaching is already present: diverse forces must be guided, not forced.

When Arjuna lifts his gaze and sees who stands on the field — his teachers, cousins, friends, and kin — something inside him breaks open. His will collapses. His bow feels suddenly heavy. He is torn between duty and compassion, past and future, action and restraint. His inner world becomes a chorus of competing truths, each one demanding allegiance. This is the Sevens' moment of testing — the recognition that purposeful action requires navigating diversity, not denying it.

Krishna, his charioteer and guide, does not command him to fight. He does not shame him for his hesitation. Instead, he invites him into dialogue. The battlefield becomes a threshold space, suspended between action and reflection. Together they explore the nature of duty, the weight of grief, the meaning of justice, and the responsibility of power. Their conversation becomes a sacred negotiation — a process of compromise, integration, and mutual understanding. Krishna offers wisdom, but Arjuna must interpret it through his own experience. Harmony is not imposed; it is co-created.

As Arjuna listens, something shifts. The conflicting parts of himself begin to align. He does not silence his grief or deny his compassion. Instead, he weaves them into his purpose. The two horses — impulse and restraint, emotion and reason — begin to move together. The reins in his hands feel different now: not instruments of control, but channels of coordination.

Arjuna lifts his bow, not out of aggression, but out of clarity. His action becomes purposeful, integrated, and freely chosen.

Krishna and Arjuna's story teaches that willpower is not domination, but coordination — the ability to guide diverse forces toward a shared direction. The Chariot reminds us that purposeful action arises from inner agreement, not inner suppression. The Sevens remind us that tests are invitations to refine our values, negotiate our truths, and move forward with integrity.

Just like the Chariot and the Sevens, Krishna and Arjuna show us that progress is not the victory of one force over another, but the harmony of many. They reveal that diversity — within ourselves and between us — is not an obstacle to movement, but the very material from which purposeful action is shaped.

## Closing Reflection

The Chariot stands strong, harnessing opposing forces with discipline and respect. The Sevens mirror his lesson in everyday life – through courage, fantasy, responsibility, and patience. Together, they remind us that progress is not easy, but it is possible.

In psychology and behavioral science, we see that willpower is not a single force but a coordination of competing impulses — much like the Chariot's steeds. Progress emerges when the mind learns to regulate tension rather than eliminate it, turning inner conflict into forward motion.

Cosmically, he echoes the momentum of celestial bodies: motion sustained not by perfection, but by balance. Planets stay their course through the interplay of gravity and velocity — a reminder that mastery is less about force and more about alignment with the energies already in motion.

And in our cultural moment, where speed is often mistaken for success and overwhelm is a constant companion, the Chariot offers a steadier truth. Perseverance is the path to mastery. To stand firm, to choose wisely, to act with integrity, and to adapt with patience is to move forward with strength and resilience — not through domination, but through disciplined direction.

## Journaling prompt

*Where do you need to assert direction and willpower to move forward with clarity?*

# Strength and the Eights

## Courage, Mastery, and the Power of Inner Resources

*"Accept that your base instincts exist, draw determination from your passion, and recognize the same in others, so that you may serve a higher state of purpose."*

*— Excerpt from Tarot Well Done*

## Strength as Number Eight: The Archetype of Inner Fortitude

Strength is the eighth card of the Major Arcana, and the first to explicitly embody one of the four essential virtues. It represents courage, resilience, and the ability to master one's instincts with compassion rather than force. The woman in white robes, adorned with flowers, calmly holds the lion's jaws – not through domination, but through gentleness and confidence. Strength teaches that gentleness is not weakness but discipline – the steady regulation of instinct through presence rather than force.

Psychologically, Strength reflects the stage of developing emotional intelligence – the ability to regulate impulses, act with patience, and inspire others through character. Spiritually, it embodies the principle of higher purpose: that true mastery comes from inner harmony, not coercion. Its lesson is that courage is not about brute force, but about resilience, compassion, and continuous self-development.

# The Eights: Movement, Mastery, and Resilience

The Minor Arcana Eights mirror Strength's archetype. Each Eight represents inner resources, movement, and perseverance – the ways we harness courage and discipline in daily life. Together, they show how resilience manifests in creativity, emotion, intellect, and material pursuits.

## Eight of Wands: Movement and Motivation

Eight wands tilt diagonally across a clear sky, buds at their tips. The Eight of Wands represents change, movement, and motivation. It is the fire of resilience – the moment when inspiration becomes action.

Psychologically, this card reflects the importance of momentum and the discipline to follow through. Spiritually, it mirrors

Strength's lesson that courage requires both inspiration and action. The test is to align passion with purpose, and to keep moving even when obstacles arise.

## Eight of Cups: Emotional Intelligence and Departure

A cloaked figure walks away from stacked cups beneath a solar eclipse. The Eight of Cups represents emotional intelligence, departure, and the bravery to leave what is familiar. It is the water of resilience – the moment when intuition guides us into the unknown.

Psychologically, this card reflects the challenge of trusting oneself to make difficult emotional choices. Spiritually, it mirrors Strength's lesson that courage is not only about facing danger – it is about leaving behind comfort when growth requires it. The test is to move forward with patience and tempered emotions.

## Eight of Swords: Restriction and Self-Reliance

A blindfolded woman stands bound among swords, head bowed. The Eight of Swords represents restriction, entrapment, and the perception of powerlessness. It is the air of resilience – the moment when intellect must be used to escape self-imposed limitations.

Psychologically, this card reflects the challenge of overcoming fear and self-doubt. Spiritually, it mirrors Strength's lesson that courage is about self-awareness – the recognition that freedom begins with belief. The test is whether we choose to remain trapped by fear or activate resilience to move forward.

**Eight of Pentacles: Skill and Perseverance**

A craftsman carves pentacles into coins, seated on a wooden bench. The Eight of Pentacles represents skill, perseverance, and the investment of effort. It is the earth of resilience – the moment when mastery is achieved through diligence.

Psychologically, this card reflects the importance of investing in oneself – education, training, and persistence. Spiritually, it mirrors Strength's lesson that courage is not only about facing adversity – it is about committing to growth. The test is whether we persevere with honest effort or allow boredom and apathy to erode progress.

## Strength and the Eights Together

Strength teaches that courage and resilience are virtues of character. The Eights show how these virtues manifest in daily life:

- ❖ **Wands (Fire)**: Movement and motivation.

- ❖ **Cups (Water)**: Emotional intelligence and departure.

- ❖ **Swords (Air)**: Restriction and self-reliance.

- ❖ **Pentacles (Earth)**: Skill and perseverance.

Together, they remind us that resilience is multifaceted. Resilience is not loud – it is the quiet discipline of meeting challenges with steadiness rather than force. It can be swift action, emotional bravery, intellectual clarity, or diligent effort. Strength's lesson is that true mastery comes from inner fortitude, not external force.

## Psychological and Spiritual Resonance

From a psychological perspective, Strength and the Eights represent the stage of resilience – learning to regulate impulses, trust intuition, overcome fear, and persevere with effort. They reflect the moment when a person begins to understand that inner steadiness is not innate but cultivated through repeated encounters with vulnerability. This psychological deepening naturally opens into the spiritual dimension, because the work of resilience is inseparable from the deeper truth that courage arises from alignment, not force.

From a spiritual perspective, Strength and the Eights embody the principle of mastery: that courage is not about domination, but about harmony with self and others. Where psychology describes how resilience forms, spirituality describes what it is for – revealing that true strength is expressed not through control, but through presence, patience, and compassion.

Strength reminds us that courage is sacred. The Eights remind us that resilience is practical. Together, they reveal that mastery is achieved through the steady integration of effort and gentleness, and that every challenge becomes an invitation to meet ourselves with greater honesty and care.

## Jesus and the Woman Who Bled – Christian Tradition

The story of Strength begins in a crowded street. The air is thick with dust and heat as Jesus walks through a throng of people pressing close on every side. Voices rise and fall around him — merchants calling out, children weaving through the crowd, sandals scraping against stone. Amid this noise, a woman moves quietly, almost invisibly, toward him.

She has suffered from bleeding for twelve years. She has spent everything she had on physicians. She has been pushed to the margins of her community, considered unclean, left to endure her pain in isolation. Her body is tired. Her spirit is thin. Yet she keeps moving. This is the Eights' first teaching: endurance in the face of long-term hardship, the quiet strength required to keep walking when nothing seems to change.

The woman reaches out and touches the hem of Jesus' garment. Her fingers barely graze the fabric. She does not grasp or demand; she simply reaches with hope — a small, trembling act that carries the weight of twelve years. Her strength is not loud. It is the courage to act despite exhaustion, shame, and fear.

Jesus feels power go out from him and stops. The crowd stills around him. He does not rebuke her. He does not pull away. Instead, he turns with gentleness and asks who touched him. His question is not for information but for recognition — an invitation for her to step out of hiding, to be seen.

Trembling, the woman comes forward. Her breath catches. She expects judgment, perhaps anger. But Jesus meets her with compassion. He calls her "daughter," restoring her dignity and belonging in a single word. Her healing is not only physical; it is relational. Jesus' strength is not forceful; it is the power to see, to affirm, to restore. This is the essence of the Strength card: gentleness that transforms what fear cannot.

The woman's twelve-year endurance mirrors the Eights' teaching: transformation often requires sustained effort, repeated attempts, and the courage to reach out again and again. Jesus' response shows that true strength is not domination but presence — the ability to meet suffering with compassion, to hold space for healing without coercion.

Jesus and the woman with the issue of blood teach that strength is relational, that endurance is sacred, and that healing often begins with the smallest act of courage. Just like Strength and the Eights, their story reveals that gentleness can restore what force cannot, and that long-term suffering can be transformed through compassion, recognition, and steady, patient faith.

## Closing Reflection

Strength shows a woman calmly subduing a lion, embodying courage and compassion. The Eights mirror her lesson in everyday life – through movement, departure, self-reliance, and perseverance. Together, they remind us that resilience is not about force – it is about inner fortitude.

Biology teaches us that calm is not the absence of fear but the regulation of it. The nervous system learns stability through repeated acts of grounded presence, and Strength reflects this quiet mastery — the way gentleness can soothe the body into courage more effectively than brute force ever could.

Cosmically, she echoes the forces that shape stars from chaos: pressure met with patience, intensity held with grace. Creation itself requires containment, not aggression — a reminder that true power is steady, not explosive.

And in our cultural moment, where strength is often equated with dominance or relentless productivity, this archetype offers a softer, truer form of resilience. Courage is the foundation of mastery. To act with patience, to trust intuition, to overcome fear, and to invest in growth is to live with resilience and purpose — not by overpowering life, but by meeting it with an open, unwavering heart.

## Journaling prompt

*How can you approach a current challenge with compassion and inner resilience rather than force?*

# The Hermit and the Nines

## Reflection, Culmination, and the Wisdom of Experience

*"You have travelled a long way, but the journey is not yet over. Stop to reflect upon everything you have learned, all that you are. The path you have followed is uniquely yours, the culmination of your past and your quest for what lies ahead, is the continuance of your journey."*

*– Excerpt from Tarot Well Done*

## The Hermit as Number Nine: The Archetype of Reflection

The Hermit is the ninth card of the Major Arcana, embodying solitude, prudence, and wisdom. He stands alone, lantern raised, illuminating the path ahead. His presence reminds us that growth requires reflection, and that wisdom is born from experience.

Psychologically, the Hermit reflects the stage of introspection – the ability to pause, evaluate, and learn from the past. Spiritually, he embodies the virtue of prudence: the careful discernment that guides all other virtues. His lesson is that solitude is not isolation, but an opportunity to gather insight and prepare for the journey ahead.

## The Nines: Culmination, Introspection, and Endurance

The Minor Arcana Nines mirror the Hermit's archetype. Each Nine represents culmination, introspection, or endurance – the near end of a cycle, when wisdom is gathered from repeated experiences. Together, they show how reflection manifests in creativity, emotion, intellect, and material pursuits.

### Nine of Wands: Courage and Resilience

A man stands on a solid platform, wand in hand, with eight others behind him. The Nine of Wands represents courage, resilience, and determination. It is the fire of introspection – the moment when past battles provide strength for future challenges.

Psychologically, this card reflects the importance of perseverance and learning from adversity. Spiritually, it mirrors the Hermit's lesson that wisdom comes from endurance. The bandaged head reminds us that scars are not signs of weakness – they are evidence of resilience.

## Nine of Cups: Gratitude and Contentment

A man sits proudly on a bench, encircled by cups. The Nine of Cups represents comfort, satisfaction, and emotional fulfillment. It is the water of introspection – the moment when gratitude and contentment arise from lived experience.

Psychologically, this card reflects the importance of appreciating victories, however small. Spiritually, it mirrors the Hermit's lesson that wisdom includes gratitude. The elevated cups remind us that emotional security is achieved by honoring both dreams and reality.

## Nine of Swords: Anxiety and Perspective

A man sits upright in bed, overwhelmed by worry, swords lined behind him. The Nine of Swords represents anxiety, nightmares, and negative thoughts. It is the air of introspection – the moment when the mind is tested by fear.

Psychologically, this card reflects the challenge of managing anxiety and obsessive thoughts. Spiritually, it mirrors the Hermit's lesson that reflection must include facing shadows. The patterned quilt reminds us that even in darkness, possibilities for hope and recovery remain.

## Nine of Pentacles: Independence and Self-Attainment

A woman stands in a vineyard, bird perched on her hand, coins at her feet. The Nine of Pentacles represents independence, sovereignty, and self-sufficiency. It is the earth of introspection – the moment when prosperity is achieved through self-investment.

Psychologically, this card reflects the importance of self-reliance and appreciation of personal achievement. Spiritually, it mirrors the Hermit's lesson that wisdom includes sovereignty. The vineyard reminds us that abundance is cultivated through conscious effort and respect for nature.

# The Hermit and the Nines Together

The Hermit teaches that reflection and prudence guide growth. The Nines show how culmination and introspection manifest in daily life:

- ❖ **Wands (Fire)**: Courage and resilience.

- ❖ **Cups (Water)**: Contentment and gratitude.

- ❖ **Swords (Air)**: Anxiety and perspective.

- ❖ **Pentacles (Earth)**: Independence and self-attainment.

Together, they remind us that wisdom is multifaceted. It can be resilience, gratitude, perspective, or sovereignty. The Hermit's lesson is that reflection transforms experience into insight. Reflection flourishes in solitude, not isolation – in the quiet space where experience can settle into wisdom.

## Psychological and Spiritual Resonance

From a psychological perspective, the Hermit and the Nines represent the stage of introspection – learning to pause, reflect, and integrate lessons. They reflect the moment when a person begins to understand that insight arises not only from experience, but from the willingness to sit with that experience long enough for meaning to emerge. This psychological turning inward naturally opens into the spiritual dimension, because the work of reflection is inseparable from the deeper truth that wisdom grows in silence, patience, and presence.

From a spiritual perspective, the Hermit and the Nines embody the principle of prudence: that wisdom is achieved through careful discernment and endurance. Where psychology describes how introspection forms, spirituality describes what it is for – revealing that solitude is not withdrawal, but a return to the inner source from which clarity arises.

The Hermit reminds us that solitude is sacred because it reconnects us to ourselves, while isolation disconnects us from everything. The Nines remind us that culmination is meaningful. Together, they reveal that reflection is the bridge between past and future, the space where experience becomes understanding and understanding becomes direction.

## Siddhartha's Enlightenment – Buddhist Tradition

The story begins with Siddhartha, a prince who walks away from everything he has ever known. The palace gates close behind him with a soft echo, and the night air feels different on his skin — cooler, wider, unmediated. He leaves his wealth, his lineage, and the identity shaped for him since birth. What pulls him forward is a question he cannot ignore: What is the nature of suffering, and how can it be eased?

His departure is not rejection but devotion — a willingness to step into solitude in search of truth. This is the Nines' first teaching: the path of refinement begins when we turn inward.

Siddhartha studies with teachers, practices austerities, and disciplines his body and mind. He fasts until his ribs show. He meditates until his limbs tremble. He pushes himself to the edge of endurance, believing that wisdom must be earned through struggle. But the more he strives, the further truth seems to slip away. His breath grows thin. His vision blurs. Exhausted, he realizes that extremes cannot reveal what lies at the center.

He sits beneath a fig tree — later called the Bodhi tree — and vows not to rise until he understands. The ground is cool beneath him. The leaves above rustle softly. This is the Hermit's essence: stillness as strength, solitude as devotion.

As Siddhartha sits, Mara approaches — not as a single figure, but as a tide of inner weather. Fear coils in the shadows. Desire flickers like heat on the horizon. Illusion whispers in familiar tones. Mara sends visions of terror, temptation, and doubt. But Siddhartha does not fight them. He does not flee. He meets each vision with calm awareness, neither grasping nor resisting. His strength is quiet, steady, inward.

The Nines remind us that the final stretch of any journey is often the most demanding — the moment when old patterns rise in one last attempt to pull us back.

Through the long night, Siddhartha remains present. His breath deepens. His mind clears. At the moment when Mara's illusions surge strongest, Siddhartha touches the earth with one hand, calling it to witness his intention. The earth responds — not with words, but with a subtle shift, a grounding presence. The illusions dissolve.

As dawn breaks, the first light spills across the horizon. Siddhartha sees clearly for the first time: the nature of suffering, the path to liberation, the interconnectedness of all beings. He becomes the Buddha — not through conquest, but through clarity. His enlightenment is not an escape from the world, but a deeper understanding of it.

The Buddha does not remain in solitude forever. After his awakening, he rises from beneath the tree and returns to the world, carrying the light he found within. This is the Hermit's final teaching: illumination is meant to be shared, not hoarded. The Nines remind us that completion is not an ending, but a threshold — the moment before wisdom becomes service.

The Buddha's story teaches that solitude is not isolation, but a sacred space for integration. The Hermit reminds us that truth emerges when we are willing to sit with ourselves. The Nines remind us that refinement requires patience, endurance, and the courage to face what arises in the quiet. His myth reveals that inner light is not given; it is uncovered — through stillness, presence, and the willingness to walk the path alone until clarity dawns.

Just like the Hermit and the Nines, the Buddha shows us that wisdom is a journey inward, that illumination is a slow unfolding, and that the light we find in solitude becomes a gift we carry back into the world.

## Closing Reflection

The Hermit stands alone, lantern raised, embodying prudence and wisdom. The Nines mirror his lesson in everyday life —

through resilience, gratitude, anxiety, and independence. Together, they remind us that reflection is not about retreat – it is about integration.

Neuroscience shows that insight often emerges in moments of solitude, when the brain shifts into its default mode network — the quiet internal landscape where memories reorganize and meaning takes shape. The Hermit reflects this inner architecture, reminding us that clarity is not forced; it arises when the mind is given room to breathe.

Cosmically, he echoes the solitary stars that guide travellers across vast distances. A single point of light can orient an entire journey, not through brightness alone but through constancy. His lantern is that steady signal — a reminder that illumination often comes from the smallest, most consistent sources.

And in our cultural moment, where constant connection is expected and silence is often mistaken for absence, the Hermit offers a different kind of presence. Wisdom is born from experience. To pause, to reflect, to endure, and to appreciate is to live with insight and purpose — not by withdrawing from life, but by integrating its lessons with honesty and care.

## Journaling prompt

*What space of solitude or reflection could help you reconnect with your own wisdom?*

# Wheel of Fortune and the Tens

## Cycles, Completion, and the Turning of Destiny

*"As your life journey continues, the ever-turning wheel of destiny is in motion. At this halfway point in the voyage, comes a time to travel beyond the material outer self and discover a spiritual inner world of experiences that will culminate to shape you as you continue your journey."*

*– Excerpt from Tarot Well Done*

## Wheel of Fortune as Number Ten: The Archetype of Cycles

The Wheel of Fortune is the tenth card of the Major Arcana, marking the halfway point in the Fool's journey. It represents fate, cycles, and change – the turning of destiny invites us inward as much as outward. The wheel reminds us that life is cyclical: endings give way to beginnings, and fortune shifts between good and bad.

Psychologically, the Wheel reflects the stage of transition – the recognition that life is shaped by both choice and circumstance. Spiritually, it embodies the principle of destiny: that karma and free will intertwine to guide our path. Its lesson is that change is inevitable, and that wisdom lies in embracing cycles with openness.

# The Tens: Completion, Transition, and Legacy

The Minor Arcana Tens mirror the Wheel's archetype. Each Ten represents completion, transition, or legacy – the end of a cycle and the beginning of another. Together, they show how destiny manifests in creativity, emotion, intellect, and material pursuits.

## Ten of Wands: Burden and Responsibility

A man struggles to carry ten wands, vision obscured, heading toward a distant dwelling. The Ten of Wands represents burden, responsibility, and the weight of completion. It is the fire of cycles – the moment when effort culminates in achievement, but at the cost of strain.

Psychologically, this card reflects the challenge of carrying too much alone. Spiritually, it mirrors the Wheel's lesson that cycles demand discernment: not every burden must be borne. The test is whether we delegate, release, or persist to completion.

## Ten of Cups: Harmony and Fulfillment

A family rejoices beneath a rainbow of cups, dwelling in harmony. The Ten of Cups represents emotional prosperity, peace, and love. It is the water of cycles – the moment when relationships reach fulfillment, and joy is shared.

Psychologically, this card reflects the importance of gratitude and trust in relationships. Spiritually, it mirrors the Wheel's lesson that harmony is earned through both rain and sunshine. The rainbow reminds us that joy follows challenge, and that cycles of emotion culminate in love.

## Ten of Swords: Ending and Renewal

A man lies pinned by ten swords, sky shifting from yellow to black. The Ten of Swords represents defeat, death, and the end of a cycle. It is the air of cycles – the moment when intellect confronts finality, and renewal begins.

Psychologically, this card reflects the pain of endings and the necessity of letting go. Spiritually, it mirrors the Wheel's lesson that endings are not absolute – they are transitions. The dawn beyond the darkness reminds us that rebirth follows loss.

**Ten of Pentacles: Legacy and Continuity**

A family gathers at the entrance of a grand dwelling, coins arranged in the Tree of Life. The Ten of Pentacles represents wealth, legacy, and intergenerational continuity. It is the earth of cycles – the moment when material prosperity culminates in legacy.

Psychologically, this card reflects the importance of family, structure, and succession. Spiritually, it mirrors the Wheel's lesson that destiny extends beyond the individual. The Tree of Life reminds us that prosperity is shared, and that legacy is the continuation of cycles. Cycles don't just end, they reorganize us.

# Wheel of Fortune and the Tens Together

The Wheel teaches that fate and cycles guide destiny. The Tens show how completion manifests in daily life:

- ❖ **Wands (Fire)**: Burden and responsibility.

- ❖ **Cups (Water)**: Harmony and fulfillment.

- ❖ **Swords (Air)**: Ending and renewal.

- ❖ **Pentacles (Earth)**: Legacy and continuity.

Together, they remind us that endings are beginnings, and that cycles are the rhythm of life. The Wheel's lesson is that destiny is not static – it turns, transforms, and renews.

## Psychological and Spiritual Resonance

From a psychological perspective, the Wheel and the Tens represent the stage of completion – learning to release burdens, celebrate harmony, accept endings, and honor legacy. They reflect the moment when a person begins to understand that culmination is not a stopping point but a turning point, a shift from what has been carried to what can now be released. This psychological recognition naturally opens into the spiritual dimension, because the experience of completion is inseparable from the deeper truth that life moves in cycles rather than straight lines.

From a spiritual perspective, the Wheel and the Tens embody the principle of cycles: that destiny is shaped by both karma and choice, and that endings are gateways to beginnings. Where psychology describes how completion unfolds, spirituality describes what it is part of – revealing that every ending participates in a larger rhythm of renewal, transition, and return.

The Wheel reminds us that change is inevitable. The Tens remind us that completion is meaningful because it prepares the ground for what comes next. Together, they reveal that destiny is lived through cycles of burden, joy, loss, and legacy, and that each cycle invites us to meet change with awareness rather than resistance.

# Ragnarök – Norse Mythology

The story of Ragnarök begins with a prophecy whispered through the nine worlds — a sound like wind moving through roots, like distant thunder rolling beneath the earth. A great cycle will end, and another will begin. The gods know the signs. The ground will shudder. The sun will dim. Old bonds will snap like frozen branches. Yet they cannot prevent what is coming.

In Norse myth, fate is not a punishment but a rhythm — a turning of the cosmic wheel that no one, not even the gods, can escape. This is the Tens' first teaching: every cycle reaches fullness, and every fullness must give way.

As the prophecy unfolds, the world enters Fimbulwinter — three endless winters with no summer between. Snow falls in relentless sheets. The air grows sharp enough to cut. Crops fail beneath the frozen soil. Families fracture under the weight of hunger. The bonds of kinship dissolve as survival narrows the heart.

The Wheel turns, and fortune shifts. What once sustained life now withers. What once seemed stable begins to crack. The gods prepare, not with denial, but with a solemn acceptance. They know that endings are woven into the fabric of existence.

When the final battle arrives, the forces of chaos rise.

Fenrir breaks his chains with a roar that shakes the sky.

Jörmungandr thrashes from the sea, poison steaming from its jaws.

Loki leads the giants across the rainbow bridge, its colors splintering under their weight.

The gods meet them on the field of Vigrid, a plain so vast it swallows the horizon. Odin faces Fenrir. Thor confronts the serpent. Freyr battles the fire giant Surtr. Each god steps into their fate with courage, knowing the cycle must complete itself. This is the Wheel's teaching: fortune rises and falls, and no one stands outside the turning.

The battle is fierce.

Odin is swallowed whole.

Thor slays the serpent but collapses from its venom.

Freyr falls beneath Surtr's blade.

Heimdall and Loki destroy each other in a final, blinding clash.

The world burns as Surtr's fire sweeps across the land. Mountains crumble. Seas boil. The sky splits open. This is the Tens' moment of culmination — the fullness before release, the ending that clears the way for what comes next.

But Ragnarök is not annihilation. It is transformation.

When the flames subside, the earth rises from the sea, green and renewed. Rivers flow again. Seeds long buried begin to sprout.

Two humans, Líf and Lífthrasir, emerge from the shelter of the world tree, blinking in the new light. Baldr returns from the underworld, bringing reconciliation and warmth. A new sun rises, born from the old.

The Wheel turns again.

Ragnarök teaches that cycles are sacred — that creation and destruction are not opposites, but partners in the dance of renewal. The Wheel of Fortune reminds us that change is inevitable, that fortune shifts, and that our task is not to resist the turning but to meet it with humility and courage. The Tens remind us that completion is not an ending, but a threshold — the moment when one story closes and another begins.

Just like the Wheel of Fortune and the Tens, Ragnarök shows us that endings are fertile, that loss clears the ground for new life, and that every cycle, no matter how vast or devastating, carries within it the promise of renewal. It reveals that the world does not end — it transforms, and we transform with it.

## Closing Reflection

The Wheel of Fortune turns, carrying us through cycles of fate and change. The Tens mirror its lesson in everyday life – through burden, harmony, endings, and legacy. Together, they remind us that completion is not final – it is transition.

In nature, cycles are fundamental. Biology moves through phases of growth, decay, and renewal; even the brain reorganizes itself through periods of disruption and integration. The Wheel reflects this living intelligence — the way change reshapes us, not as punishment, but as preparation for what comes next.

Cosmically, it echoes the great rotations that structure the universe: planets orbiting stars, stars orbiting galactic centers, galaxies drifting through expanding space. Nothing stands still. Motion is the rule, and every ending is simply a shift in trajectory.

And in our cultural moment — where certainty is prized and change often feels like instability — the Wheel offers a steadier truth. Destiny is cyclical. To embrace burden, to celebrate harmony, to accept endings, and to honor legacy is to live with wisdom and resilience — not by resisting the turn, but by learning to move with it.

## Journaling prompt

*What cycle or change are you currently experiencing, and how might you embrace its lessons?*

# Justice and the Knights
## Truth, Action, and the Testing of Integrity

*"To form a preconceived idea of what is, and then forever call it an experience, is flawed. You must first experience yourself, and second experience others, and then, with the clarity of all experiences you will travel forward into righteousness."*

*– Excerpt from Tarot Well Done*

## Justice as Number Eleven: The Archetype of Truth

Justice is the eleventh card of the Major Arcana, and the third to embody an essential virtue. She represents fairness, accountability, and clear insight – the ability to perceive situations with depth and act with integrity. Justice teaches that fairness is not the same as equality. Equality gives everyone the same, while fairness gives each person what is needed to restore balance. Unlike the blindfolded justice of the legal system, the tarot's Justice card insists on seeing clearly before judgment is made.

Psychologically, Justice reflects the stage of moral development – the weighing of cause and effect, the recognition that every choice carries consequence. Spiritually, she embodies the principle of truth: that clarity must guide action, and fairness is the measure of wisdom. Her lesson is that righteousness is not abstract – it is lived through decisions and deeds.

## The Knights: Agents of Action and Testing of Values

The Minor Arcana Knights mirror Justice's archetype. Each Knight represents movement, action, and the testing of values – the ways in which principles are put into practice. Together, they show how truth and accountability manifest in creativity, emotion, intellect, and material pursuits.

### Knight of Wands: Passion and Impulse

A flamboyant young knight rides a rearing horse, wand raised, eyes unfocused. The Knight of Wands represents passion, enthusiasm, and impulsive energy. It is the fire of testing values – the moment when desire drives action, but accountability must temper recklessness.

Psychologically, this card reflects the challenge of balancing excitement with purpose. Spiritually, it mirrors Justice's lesson that passion must align with truth. The test is whether energy is used constructively or wasted in volatility.

## Knight of Cups: Romance and Idealism

A knight rides elegantly, chalice extended, horse prancing. The Knight of Cups represents romance, idealism, and emotional pursuit. It is the water of testing values – the moment when love inspires action, but sincerity must be proven.

Psychologically, this card reflects the challenge of acting on emotional ideals without losing grounding. Spiritually, it mirrors Justice's lesson that sincerity must be tested by fairness. The test is whether emotional pursuit honors truth or succumbs to illusion.

## Knight of Swords: Intellect and Aggression

A knight charges at full speed, sword raised, cape billowing. The Knight of Swords represents intellect, determination, and aggressive pursuit of ideals. It is the air of testing values – the moment when clarity drives action, but fairness must temper force.

Psychologically, this card reflects the challenge of balancing intellect with compassion. Spiritually, it mirrors Justice's lesson that truth must be pursued with integrity, not cruelty. The test is whether intellect serves justice or becomes rigid extremism.

**Knight of Pentacles: Diligence and Responsibility**

A knight sits steady on a black horse, pentacle in hand, beside a ploughed field. The Knight of Pentacles represents diligence, loyalty, and responsibility. It is the earth of testing values – the moment when patience and persistence prove integrity.

Psychologically, this card reflects the importance of responsibility and steady effort. Spiritually, it mirrors Justice's lesson that fairness requires diligence. The test is whether persistence serves truth or becomes stagnation.

## Justice and the Knights Together

Justice teaches that truth and fairness guide action. The Knights show how values are tested in daily life:

- ❖ **Wands (Fire)**: Passion and impulse.

- ❖ **Cups (Water)**: Romance and idealism.

- ❖ **Swords (Air)**: Intellect and aggression.

- ❖ **Pentacles (Earth)**: Diligence and responsibility.

Together, they remind us that action is the test of integrity. Justice's lesson is that fairness must temper passion, idealism, intellect, and diligence. Fairness requires discernment – not sameness, but proportionate correction.

## Psychological and Spiritual Resonance

From a psychological perspective, Justice and the Knights represent the stage of accountability – learning to act with integrity, balance, and fairness. They reflect the moment when a person begins to understand that choices carry consequences, and that values must be lived rather than merely believed. This psychological awakening naturally opens into the spiritual dimension, because the work of accountability is inseparable from the deeper truth that truth itself is a sacred force.

From a spiritual perspective, Justice and the Knights embody the principle of truth: that clarity must guide action, and that fairness is sacred. Fairness restores balance by discerning whatever is needed to correct imbalance. Where psychology describes how accountability forms, spirituality describes what it is for – revealing that truth is not only a principle but a path, one that asks us to align our actions with what is real and right.

Justice reminds us that truth is impartial. The Knights remind us that action tests values. Together, they reveal that integrity is proven not in thought but in deed, and that every choice becomes an opportunity to bring our inner principles into the world with clarity and courage.

# The Weighing the Heart – Egyptian Mythology

The Hall of Two Truths is where the soul arrives after death to stand before the gods. The hall is vast and still, its silence deep enough to feel. A soft, unwavering light fills the space — a light that reveals everything and hides nothing. Shadows cannot cling here. Masks cannot hold. This is not a place of punishment, but of clarity.

The soul carries its heart — the ib — cupped gently in its hands. In Egyptian thought, the heart is the seat of memory, intention, and truth. It records every action, every motive, every moment of alignment or distortion. It is the truest witness of a life. This is the Knights' first teaching: integrity is lived, not declared.

Anubis, the jackal-headed guide, steps forward with quiet authority. His presence is steadying, neither harsh nor indulgent. He leads the soul to a golden scale that gleams in the stillness. On one side, he places the heart. On the other, he sets the Feather of Ma'at — the principle of truth, balance, and cosmic order.

Ma'at is not a deity of punishment; she is the rhythm by which the universe remains in harmony. To live in accordance with Ma'at is to live with clarity, reciprocity, and right relationship.

Thoth, the scribe of the gods, stands nearby with his reed pen poised above a fresh tablet. His gaze is sharp, attentive, ready to record the outcome with perfect accuracy. Osiris presides over the ceremony, calm and steady, embodying the stillness that comes when truth is allowed to speak for itself. No argument can sway the scale. No plea can alter the weight of the heart. Justice here is not imposed; it is revealed.

If the heart is light — free of the heaviness that comes from deceit, cruelty, or unintegrated action — the scale balances. A soft breeze moves through the hall, and the soul is welcomed into the Field of Reeds, a place of harmony and abundance where life continues in alignment with Ma'at.

If the heart is heavy, weighed down by what was never reconciled, the scale tips. Ammit, the Devourer, waits at the edge of the hall — part lion, part crocodile, part hippopotamus. She does not punish. She simply returns what is fragmented to the cycle, so that one day it may be made whole again. This is dissolution, not torment — a reset, not a sentence.

The Weighing of the Heart teaches that justice is not a verdict handed down from above, but a reflection of how we have lived. The Knights remind us that our daily actions shape the weight of the heart — that truth is not an idea but a practice, a way of moving through the world with courage, clarity, and care. Justice reminds us that balance is sacred, that right relationship is the foundation of harmony, and that every choice contributes to the shape of the soul.

Just like Justice and the Knights, this myth reveals that integrity is a path, not a moment. It shows us that truth is light, that alignment is freedom, and that a life lived with courage and compassion leaves the heart unburdened — ready to meet the scales without fear.

## Closing Reflection

Justice sits with sword and scales, embodying truth and fairness. The Knights mirror her lesson in everyday life — through passion, romance, intellect, and diligence. Together, they remind us that action is the measure of integrity.

Cognitive science shows that fairness is not an abstract ideal but a deeply wired instinct; the brain reacts strongly to imbalance, seeking resolution even before we can articulate why something feels wrong. Justice reflects this inner calibration — the quiet, ongoing work of aligning perception with principle.

Cosmically, she echoes the equilibrium that governs the universe. Stars maintain their form through the balance of pressure and gravity, and ecosystems thrive when forces are held in proportion. Her scales are a reminder that harmony is not passive; it is an active, dynamic state maintained through continual adjustment.

And in our cultural moment — where truth is often contested and performance can overshadow principle — Justice offers a steadying call. Truth must be lived, not only known. To act with fairness, to align passion with principle, to temper intellect with compassion, and to persist with responsibility is to embody integrity — not as a posture, but as a practice.

## Journaling prompt

*Where in your life is truth or accountability asking to be acknowledged?*

# The Hanged Man and the Queens

## Surrender, Perspective, and Embodied Wisdom

*"You are in a moment of pause, with nothing more than your free will, and the time in which to reflect on the suppositions you have been dependent upon. Acknowledge them, and what they may be worth to you, if worth anything at all."*

*– Excerpt from Tarot Well Done*

## The Hanged Man as Number Twelve: The Archetype of Surrender

The Hanged Man is the twelfth card of the Major Arcana, representing surrender, acceptance, and the willingness to see life from a new perspective. Hanging upside down, haloed in golden light, he embodies receptivity – the pause that allows transformation. His lesson is that enlightenment often comes not through struggle, but through letting go. The Hanged Man also teaches that surrender is rarely comfortable – it asks us to release control before we feel ready, trusting that clarity will emerge in the pause.

Psychologically, the Hanged Man reflects the stage of suspension – moments when progress requires patience, reflection, and openness to new viewpoints. Spiritually, he embodies the principle of surrender: that wisdom is found in yielding, not resisting. His calm posture reminds us that receptivity is not weakness – it is strength in waiting.

## The Queens: Embodiment, Receptivity, and Influence

The Minor Arcana Queens mirror the Hanged Man's archetype. Each Queen represents embodiment, receptivity, and influence – the ways wisdom and patience manifest in creativity, emotion, intellect, and material pursuits. Together, they show how surrender and perspective are lived through embodied presence.

### Queen of Wands: Inspiration and Action

A regal woman sits confidently, sunflower in hand, wand upright, black cat at her feet. The Queen of Wands represents inspiration, warmth, and vibrancy. She is the fire of receptivity – the moment when passion is embodied and delegated through influence.

Psychologically, this card reflects the ability to inspire others to act. Spiritually, it mirrors the Hanged Man's lesson that receptivity can be active – embodying passion while allowing others to carry it forward. The test is whether inspiration is used to empower, or to control.

## Queen of Cups: Intuition and Compassion

A gentle woman gazes at a closed chalice, seated by rippling waters. The Queen of Cups represents intuition, sensitivity, and emotional abundance. She is the water of receptivity – the moment when compassion is embodied and offered as safe harbor.

Psychologically, this card reflects the importance of empathy and emotional intelligence. Spiritually, it mirrors the Hanged Man's lesson that surrender requires openness of heart. The test is whether compassion is offered freely, or whether vulnerability becomes frailty.

## Queen of Swords: Strategy and Truth

A majestic woman sits alert, sword upright, hand extended in welcome. The Queen of Swords represents intellect, perception, and communication. She is the air of receptivity – the moment when truth is embodied and strategy guides outcomes.

Psychologically, this card reflects the importance of clarity and focus. Spiritually, it mirrors the Hanged Man's lesson that perspective requires discernment. The test is whether intellect is used to illuminate truth or manipulate others.

**Queen of Pentacles: Prosperity and Nurturing**

A serene woman gazes at a coin in her lap, surrounded by fertile landscape. The Queen of Pentacles represents practicality, nurturing, and material abundance. She is the earth of receptivity – the moment when prosperity is embodied and managed with care.

Psychologically, this card reflects the importance of valuing resources and cultivating wellbeing. Spiritually, it mirrors the Hanged Man's lesson that surrender includes trust in the material world. The test is whether prosperity is nurtured for growth or hoarded in fear.

# The Hanged Man and the Queens Together

The Hanged Man teaches that surrender and perspective guide transformation. The Queens show how receptivity manifests in daily life:

- ❖ **Wands (Fire)**: Inspiration and action.

- ❖ **Cups (Water)**: Intuition and compassion.

- ❖ **Swords (Air)**: Strategy and truth.

- ❖ **Pentacles (Earth)**: Prosperity and nurturing.

Together, they remind us that wisdom is embodied, not abstract. The Hanged Man's lesson is that receptivity is strength, and the Queens embody this truth in their domains. Receptivity often begins with discomfort – the willingness to pause long enough for a new perspective to take root.

## Psychological and Spiritual Resonance

From a psychological perspective, the Hanged Man and the Queens represent the stage of receptivity – learning to pause, embody wisdom, and influence with patience. They reflect the moment when a person begins to understand that stillness is not passivity but a form of active awareness, a way of creating space for deeper insight. This psychological softening naturally opens into the spiritual dimension, because the work of receptivity is inseparable from the deeper truth that perspective is gained not by grasping, but by allowing.

From a spiritual perspective, the Hanged Man and the Queens embody the principle of surrender: that perspective is gained through openness, and that influence is most powerful when embodied with integrity. Where psychology describes how receptivity forms, spirituality describes what it is for – revealing that surrender is not collapse, but a conscious yielding that makes room for wisdom to emerge.

The Hanged Man reminds us that surrender is sacred because it asks us to soften into uncertainty, not escape it. The Queens remind us that embodiment is influential. Together, they reveal that wisdom is lived through receptivity and presence, and that true influence arises from the steadiness we cultivate within.

## Tara Pauses the World – Buddhist Tradition

The story of the Hanged Man begins with a young woman deep in meditation, her spine tall, her breath steady, her mind luminous. The air around her is quiet, warm with the faint scent of incense. She has practiced for countless lifetimes, refining her intention, her compassion, her clarity, and her grounded presence. She sits not to escape the world, but to understand it – to feel its truth without distortion.

This is the Queens' first teaching: true power arises from inner sovereignty, not outer control.

As she meditates, something within her opens. A profound realization dawns like light rising behind her closed eyes. The path before her becomes clear — she could step beyond the cycle of birth and death, entering the freedom she has long sought. The threshold is right there, shimmering, inviting.

But as she rises toward enlightenment, she hears the cries of the world: beings trapped in fear, grief, confusion, and longing. Their suffering moves through her like a tide, tugging at the deepest part of her heart. She cannot turn away. In that moment, she makes a vow that reverses the usual direction of spiritual aspiration. She chooses not to leave. She chooses to stay. She suspends her own liberation until all beings are free.

This is the Hanged Man's essence: a voluntary pause that transforms the one who chooses it. Her vow ignites a fire within her — the fire of enlightened intention. She becomes Tara, the embodiment of inspired action born from stillness. This is the Queen of Wands: the flame that moves only after it has listened.

Her compassion deepens into an oceanic presence. She feels the suffering of the world without drowning in it, holding each being with tenderness and clarity. This is the Queen of Cups: intuition that flows from an open, sovereign heart.

Her mind becomes a blade of truth. She sees through illusion, fear, and distortion, cutting through confusion with gentle precision. This is the Queen of Swords: clarity born from surrender, discernment born from stillness.

Her body becomes rooted like a tree. She stands with the steadiness of the earth, nurturing growth, offering protection, honoring the cycles of becoming. This is the Queen of Pentacles: grounded wisdom, patient and enduring.

Tara embodies all four elements because she has surrendered the need to choose one path over another. Her power is not divided; it is integrated. She steps forward with one foot extended — always ready to act — yet she remains anchored in the stillness that gave birth to her vow. She is motion and pause, fire and water, air and earth, all held in balance.

Tara's story teaches that surrender is not weakness but devotion, that stillness is not stagnation but transformation, and that the deepest wisdom arises when we allow ourselves to hang between what was and what will be. The Hanged Man reminds us that illumination comes when we release our grip. The Queens remind us that sovereignty is an inner state, cultivated through compassion, clarity, inspiration, and grounded presence.

Just like Tara, the Hanged Man and the Queens show us that true power is receptive, that transformation begins in stillness, and that the world is changed not only by what we do, but by the depth of presence from which we do it.

## Closing Reflection

The Hanged Man hangs serenely, haloed in light, embodying surrender and perspective. The Queens mirror his lesson in everyday life – through inspiration, compassion, strategy, and nurturing. Together, they remind us that receptivity is not passive – it is powerful.

Neuroscience shows that insight often arises when the mind shifts out of effort and into openness. When we stop forcing solutions, the brain reorganizes information in the background, allowing new connections to surface. The Hanged Man reflects this quiet intelligence — the way clarity emerges when we soften our grip.

Cosmically, he echoes the suspended moments in the universe: the pause before a star ignites, the stillness between cycles, the equilibrium that precedes transformation. His inversion is not disorientation but recalibration — a reminder that perspective changes everything.

And in our cultural moment, where urgency is rewarded and stillness is often mistaken for stagnation, the Hanged Man offers a counter-rhythm. Wisdom is embodied. To inspire, to empathize, to strategize, and to nurture is to live with patience, perspective, and grace — not by pushing harder, but by allowing space for what wants to unfold.

## Journaling prompt

*What situation might benefit from you surrendering control and seeing it from a new perspective?*

# Death and the Kings

## Transformation, Mastery, and the Inevitability of Change

*"Discard that which does not serve you well and see that by surrendering the past, you may finally achieve clear sight of a future that may otherwise appear impossible."*

*– Excerpt from Tarot Well Done*

### Death as Number Thirteen: The Archetype of Transformation

Death is the thirteenth card of the Major Arcana, often misunderstood as sinister but in truth representing transformation, endings, and rebirth. It marks the inevitable close of cycles and the dawn of new beginnings. The skeletal horseman reminds us that endings are universal, touching all people regardless of status, wealth, or age.

Psychologically, Death reflects the stage of transition – the recognition that growth requires letting go. Spiritually, it embodies the principle of rebirth: that endings are not final, but gateways to renewal. Transformation often asks us to let go before we feel ready. Death's lesson is that transformation is inevitable, and that surrendering the past opens the path to the future.

## The Kings: Culmination, Mastery, and Change

The Minor Arcana Kings mirror Death's archetype. Each King represents culmination, mastery, and authority – the final stage of development within their suit. Together, they show how transformation manifests in creativity, emotion, intellect, and material pursuits.

### King of Wands: Vision and Courage

A regal man sits confidently, wand in hand, salamanders adorning his throne and cloak. The King of Wands represents vision, leadership, and courage. He is the fire of mastery – the culmination of willpower and creativity.

Psychologically, this card reflects the importance of inspiring others with bravery and vision. Spiritually, it mirrors Death's lesson that even mastery must transform. The test is whether courage evolves into arrogance, or whether vision adapts to new cycles.

## King of Cups: Emotional Mastery and Compassion

A noble man sits serenely on a throne floating on turbulent waters, chalice and scepter in hand. The King of Cups represents emotional mastery, compassion, and intuitive strength. He is the water of mastery – the culmination of emotional intelligence and spiritual yearning.

Psychologically, this card reflects the importance of stability and empathy in leadership. Spiritually, it mirrors Death's lesson that emotional mastery must evolve. The test is whether compassion deepens into renewal, or whether emotional strain erodes stability.

## King of Swords: Intellect and Justice

A regal man sits upright, sword raised, surrounded by calm skies and symbols of truth. The King of Swords represents intellect, clarity, and justice. He is the air of mastery – the culmination of knowledge and communication.

Psychologically, this card reflects the importance of truth and directness in leadership. Spiritually, it mirrors Death's lesson that even intellect must surrender to transformation. The test is whether clarity evolves into wisdom, or whether rigidity leads to downfall.

## King of Pentacles: Prosperity and Acquisition

A wealthy man sits on a throne adorned with bulls, surrounded by vines and abundance. The King of Pentacles represents prosperity, practicality, and acquisition. He is the earth of mastery – the culmination of material success and grounded stability.

Psychologically, this card reflects the importance of managing wealth with responsibility. Spiritually, it mirrors Death's lesson that material success is temporary. The test is whether prosperity transforms into legacy, or whether greed leads to corruption.

## Death and the Kings Together

Death teaches that transformation and endings are inevitable. The Kings show how mastery culminates in each domain:

- **Wands (Fire)**: Vision and courage.

- **Cups (Water)**: Emotional mastery and compassion.

- **Swords (Air)**: Intellect and justice.

- **Pentacles (Earth)**: Prosperity and acquisition.

Together, they remind us that mastery is not the end – it is the moment before transformation asks us to evolve again. Death's lesson is that even kings must surrender to change.

# Psychological and Spiritual Resonance

From a psychological perspective, Death and the Kings represent the stage of culmination – learning to master creativity, emotion, intellect, and material success, while accepting that transformation is inevitable. They reflect the moment when a person begins to understand that mastery is not a final state but a threshold, a point at which accumulated experience must be released to make room for what comes next. This psychological recognition naturally opens into the spiritual dimension, because the work of culmination is inseparable from the deeper truth that every ending carries the seed of renewal.

From a spiritual perspective, they embody the principle of rebirth: that endings are gateways to renewal, and that mastery must evolve into legacy. Where psychology describes how culmination forms, spirituality describes what it is part of – revealing that transformation is not an interruption of life's path, but its continuation in a new form.

Death reminds us that endings are sacred. The Kings remind us that mastery is temporary because life keeps moving – and wisdom is the willingness to move with it. Together, they reveal that transformation is the destiny of all, and that true mastery lies not in holding on, but in allowing ourselves to evolve with the cycles that shape us.

# The Death of Solomon – Islamic Tradition

The story of Death begins with a king whose wisdom is said to surpass that of all who came before him. Solomon rules with a sovereignty that touches every realm — humans, animals, winds, and jinn. His authority is vast, his insight unmatched, his kingdom flourishing. Yet even at the height of his power, he knows that all things move in cycles.

This is the Kings' first teaching: true authority is not ownership, but stewardship.

Solomon's fire burns bright — the fire of inspired leadership, vision, and spiritual command. He directs the winds with a gesture, speaks to birds in their own language, and governs with a clarity that ignites justice across the land. This is the King of Wands: sovereignty expressed through purpose and illumination.

His compassion runs deep. He listens to the smallest creatures, settles disputes with tenderness, and rules with a heart attuned to the needs of his people. This is the King of Cups: emotional wisdom held in steady hands.

His mind is sharp as a blade. He discerns truth from illusion, sees through deception, and governs with a clarity that cuts through confusion. This is the King of Swords: sovereignty expressed through truth and discernment.

His kingdom is prosperous, fertile, and grounded. He builds, nurtures, and sustains. His rule brings stability, abundance, and order. This is the King of Pentacles: sovereignty expressed through care for the material world.

Solomon embodies all four Kings because he holds all four elements in balance. Yet even he cannot escape the turning of the great cycle.

One day, Solomon stands in his sanctuary, leaning on his staff as he oversees the labor of the jinn. The room is quiet except for the soft hum of their work. Dust motes drift through shafts of light. Solomon's gaze is fixed on the unseen, his breath slow, his presence steady. In this moment of stillness, his life's cycle completes. His breath leaves him quietly. His body remains upright, supported by the staff. No one knows he has died.

Days pass. Then weeks. The jinn continue their work, believing their king still watches over them. But Death has already entered the room. It is not violent. It is not dramatic. It is simply the closing of a cycle — the release that comes for all beings, no matter how exalted.

At last, the staff begins to crumble. Termites, working in silence, eat through the wood until it can no longer bear the weight. The moment is small, almost tender. The staff gives way. Solomon's body falls, and only then do the jinn realize the truth: even the greatest king cannot stand forever.

This is the Death card's essence.

What has reached fullness must fall away.

What has completed its purpose must be released.

No stature, no privilege, no power can halt the turning of the cycle.

Solomon's fall is not a tragedy. It is a revelation. His death teaches that sovereignty is temporary, that leadership is a season, and that wisdom lies not in resisting endings but in accepting them with grace. The Kings remind us that authority is fulfilled when it is relinquished. Death reminds us that every cycle — even the most glorious — must eventually return to the earth.

Just like Death and the Kings, Solomon's story shows us that endings are not failures but transitions, that legacy is carried forward by those who remain, and that the measure of a life is not how long one stands, but how deeply one has served before the fall.

## Closing Reflection

Death rides forward, skeletal yet inevitable, heralding transformation and rebirth. The Kings mirror his lesson in everyday life – through vision, compassion, intellect, and prosperity. Together, they remind us that mastery is not the final destination – it is the turning point toward renewal.

Biology shows that transformation is built into every living system. Cells shed, regenerate, and reorganize; the body is in a constant state of becoming. Death reflects this natural intelligence — the way endings create the conditions for new forms of life to emerge.

Cosmically, he echoes the life cycle of stars. Even their collapse seeds the universe with the elements needed for future worlds. Nothing is wasted. Every dissolution becomes the groundwork for creation, a reminder that rebirth is woven into the fabric of existence.

And in our cultural moment — where change is often feared and identity can feel fixed — Death offers a deeper truth. Transformation is universal. To surrender the past, to evolve mastery into legacy, and to embrace rebirth is to live with wisdom and courage — not by clinging to what was, but by stepping willingly into what can be.

## Journaling prompt

*What ending or transformation in your life could open the door to renewal?*

# Temperance and the Cross-Suit Integration

## Balance, Moderation, and the Alchemy of Harmony

*"A new dawn promises new insight. Make peace with the past, moderate the present and enable your future. See things as they are and harmonize your will with that which must be, for the path is narrow and requires steady footstep."*

*— Excerpt from Tarot Well Done*

## Temperance as Number Fourteen: The Archetype of Balance

Temperance is the fourteenth card of the Major Arcana, and the fourth to embody an essential virtue. It represents moderation, self-control, and the harmonizing of opposites. The angel pouring water between chalices reminds us that balance is not passive — it is an active blending of forces, a conscious alchemy.

Psychologically, Temperance reflects the stage of integration – learning to regulate impulses, reconcile contradictions, and find equilibrium between extremes. Spiritually, it embodies the principle of harmony: that enlightenment is achieved not through excess, but through balance. Its lesson is that moderation is the path to wholeness, and that synthesis is the key to growth.

## The Cross-Suit Integration: Balance Across Domains

Unlike earlier chapters, which paired Major Arcana cards with their numerical Minor Arcana counterparts, Temperance marks a turning point. Here, the tarot begins to move beyond number relationships, drawing instead from a variety of cards across the suits that embody aspects of balance. Temperance is the alchemist of the deck, weaving together fire, water, air, and earth into a unified whole.

### Wands (Fire): Moderated Passion

Temperance tempers the impulsive energy of the Wands. Where the Ten of Wands shows burden, Temperance teaches moderation – channeling passion into sustainable effort rather than exhaustion.

### Cups (Water): Balanced Emotion

Temperance harmonizes the emotional flow of the Cups. Where

the Two of Cups shows union, Temperance expands this into a broader principle of emotional reciprocity – ensuring compassion does not overwhelm, but steadies relationships.

## Swords (Air): Clear Perspective

Temperance integrates intellect with empathy. Where the Six of Swords shows transition, Temperance teaches that clarity must be tempered by patience, ensuring truth is not wielded harshly but with fairness.

## Pentacles (Earth): Grounded Prosperity

Temperance roots spiritual balance in material stability. Where the Four of Pentacles shows clinging, Temperance teaches moderation – valuing prosperity without greed, grounding abundance in generosity and care.

# Temperance and the Suits Together

Temperance teaches that balance is achieved when all suits are harmonized:

- ❖ **Wands (Fire):** Passion moderated.

- ❖ **Cups (Water):** Emotion balanced.

- ❖ **Swords (Air):** Perspective clarified.

- ❖ **Pentacles (Earth):** Prosperity grounded.

Together, they remind us that harmony is not found in extremes, but in the steady blending of opposites. Temperance's lesson is that integration is the path to wholeness. It teaches that harmony is not the absence of tension, but the art of holding tension until it becomes coherence.

## Psychological and Spiritual Resonance

From a psychological perspective, Temperance represents individuation – the integration of impulses, emotions, intellect, and material concerns into a balanced self. It reflects the moment when a person begins to understand that harmony is not a fixed state but an ongoing practice of aligning inner parts that once felt separate. This psychological integration naturally opens into the spiritual dimension, because the work of balancing the self is inseparable from the deeper truth that transformation arises through relationship between opposites.

From a spiritual perspective, Temperance embodies alchemy – the transformation of disparate elements into harmony, bridging heaven and earth. Where psychology describes how integration forms, spirituality describes what it is for – revealing that alchemy is not a metaphor but a lived process, one in which inner contradictions become sources of wisdom rather than conflict.

Temperance reminds us that balance is sacred. The suits remind us that integration is practical because it shapes how we act, not just how we feel. Together, they reveal that harmony is achieved through moderation and synthesis, and that the work of bringing the self into coherence is both a spiritual practice and a daily discipline.

## The Rainbow Serpent – Australian Indigenous Tradition

The story of Temperance begins in the Dreaming, when the world is still unshaped and the elements lie in quiet potential. The land is flat and pale beneath a sky without wind. The waters are still, holding the faint shimmer of possibility. The air is silent, untouched by breath or movement. Fire sleeps beneath the earth like a heartbeat waiting to begin. Nothing yet moves, but everything waits — impulses, emotions, thoughts, and instincts present but unintegrated.

This is the psyche before individuation.

Then the Rainbow Serpent stirs.

She rises from beneath the ground, her body shimmering with all colors at once — red deep as clay, blue bright as sky, gold warm as dawn. As she moves across the land, the world responds. Her belly carves the first rivers. Her coils raise mountains. Her tail shapes valleys. Her motion awakens the elements. Water flows behind her. Air swirls above her. Fire cracks open the earth in glowing seams. Soil gathers into fertile plains.

This is the first alchemy: disparate elements brought into relationship through a single unifying presence.

The Rainbow Serpent does not dominate the elements; she harmonizes them. She teaches them how to coexist — water softening earth, fire warming air, air carrying rain, earth grounding flame. Her movement is deliberate, balanced, fluid. She is neither forceful nor passive. She is the mediator, the integrator, the one who brings the world into coherence.

This is Temperance's essence: the blending of opposites into harmony, the transformation of raw potential into living balance.

As the Serpent travels, life begins to emerge. Plants root themselves in the newly formed soil, their leaves trembling in the newborn wind. Animals awaken from the earth, blinking into the light. Birds take to the sky, their wings stirring the air into song. The world becomes a tapestry of interdependent forms, each sustained by the careful equilibrium she has created. Nothing exists alone. Everything participates in the whole.

The Rainbow Serpent teaches that creation is not a single act but an ongoing process of adjustment, blending, and recalibration.

She shows that balance is not static — it is a living, breathing relationship between forces that must be tended with care. This is the psychological work of individuation: bringing impulses, emotions, intellect, and material needs into dialogue rather than conflict.

Temperance reminds us that harmony is sacred.

The suits remind us that harmony is practical.

Together, they teach that integration is both an inner alchemy and an outer practice — a way of living that honors every part of the self without letting any one part dominate.

Just like Temperance and the cross-suit integration, the Rainbow Serpent reveals that wholeness is not achieved through suppression or excess, but through the gentle blending of all that we are. She shows us that when the elements within us find balance, the world around us becomes a place where life can flourish.

## Closing Reflection

Temperance pours water between chalices, reminding us that harmony is not found in extremes but in the blending of opposites. The suits mirror her lesson – passion, emotion, intellect, and prosperity must be balanced if we are to walk the narrow path toward enlightenment.

Biology shows that systems thrive through regulation, not excess. The body maintains equilibrium through countless micro-adjustments, constantly blending signals to keep us steady. Temperance reflects this quiet intelligence — the way balance is created through ongoing, responsive calibration rather than rigid control.

Cosmically, she echoes the forces that shape the universe through fusion and equilibrium. Stars are born when opposing pressures find their point of harmony, and even galaxies form through the graceful merging of disparate energies. Her chalices mirror this cosmic dance — the art of combining elements until something new and luminous emerges.

And in our cultural moment — where polarization is common and extremes are often celebrated — Temperance offers a gentler truth. Balance is the foundation of growth. To moderate passion, to harmonize emotion, to clarify perspective, and to ground prosperity is to live with wisdom and grace — not by denying our impulses, but by blending them into a coherent, steady way of being.

## Journaling prompt

*Where do you need balance or integration between opposing forces in your life?*

# The Devil and the Shadow Aspects

## Temptation, Bondage, and the Challenge of Liberation

*"If you are trapped in the darkness, you need only find the light to be free."*

*— Excerpt from Tarot Well Done*

## The Devil as Number Fifteen: The Archetype of Shadow

The Devil is the fifteenth card of the Major Arcana, and the first to explicitly embody the shadow side of human development. Where Temperance taught balance and integration, the Devil confronts us with temptation, bondage, and the ways we become enslaved by our own desires. The chains around the figures in the card are loose — they can be slipped off at any time. The Devil's lesson is that enslavement is often self-imposed, and liberation requires vigilance and choice.

Psychologically, the Devil reflects the stage of shadow confrontation – recognizing how addictions, obsessions, and complacency distort growth. Shadow often reflects and unmet need – a longing we have pushed into the dark, where it twists itself into compulsion, fear, or fixation. Spiritually, it embodies the principle of vigilance: that enlightenment requires us to see through illusion and resist enslavement to material or emotional traps. Its lesson is that freedom begins with awareness, and that shadow must be faced before it can be transcended.

## The Shadow Aspects Across the Suits

Unlike earlier chapters, which paired Major Arcana cards with virtues or integrations, the Devil reveals how each suit can enslave us when distorted. These are the shadow aspects – the reversals that show how power becomes bondage.

### Wands (Fire): Obsession and Impulse

The fire of Wands, when distorted, becomes obsession, recklessness, and destructive passion. The Devil warns against mistaking compulsion for courage, or lust for vision.

### Cups (Water): Emotional Despair

The water of Cups, when distorted, becomes emotional dependency, despair, and toxic attachment. The Devil warns against drowning in obsession, mistaking possession for love, or allowing emotions to enslave.

## Swords (Air): Mental Cruelty

The air of Swords, when distorted, becomes manipulation, cruelty, and destructive ideologies. The Devil warns against using intellect as a weapon, enslaving others through fear or distortion of truth.

## Pentacles (Earth): Material Greed

The earth of Pentacles, when distorted, becomes greed, exploitation, and fixation on possessions. The Devil warns against mistaking wealth for worth, or allowing materialism to obscure spiritual growth.

# The Devil and the Suits Together

The Devil teaches that shadow is present in every domain:

- ❖ **Wands (Fire):** Obsession enslaves passion.

- ❖ **Cups (Water):** Despair enslaves emotion.

- ❖ **Swords (Air):** Cruelty enslaves intellect.

- ❖ **Pentacles (Earth):** Greed enslaves prosperity.

Together, they remind us that shadow is not external – it is the distortion of our own gifts. Shadow is often the place where a legitimate need has gone unacknowledged and so expresses itself in distorted form. The Devil's lesson is that vigilance is required to free ourselves from bondage.

# Psychological and Spiritual Resonance

From a psychological perspective, the Devil and the shadow suits represent the stage of vigilance – learning to recognize how our strengths can become traps when distorted. They reflect the moment when a person begins to understand that shadow is not an enemy but a signal, revealing where unmet needs or unexamined fears are shaping behaviour. This psychological alertness naturally opens into the spiritual dimension, because the work of naming distortion is inseparable from the deeper truth that awareness is the first step toward freedom.

From a spiritual perspective, they embody the principle of liberation: that freedom requires awareness, and that shadow must be faced before light can be found. Where psychology describes how distortion forms, spirituality describes what it is for – revealing that liberation is not achieved by avoidance, but by turning toward what binds us with clarity and compassion.

The Devil reminds us that bondage is often self-imposed. The suits remind us that shadow is often the unmet need beneath the distortion. Together, they reveal that liberation is achieved through awareness, vigilance, and choice, and that every encounter with shadow is an invitation to reclaim the parts of ourselves we once abandoned.

# The Qliphoth – Kabbalistic Tradition

The story of the Devil begins with a tree of light — the Tree of Life — rising like a pillar between worlds. Its branches shimmer with ten emanations of divine energy, each one glowing with its own hue: compassion warm as dawn, strength steady as stone, beauty radiant as a star, wisdom clear as running water, sovereignty bright as a crown of fire. Together they form a harmonious whole, a balanced expression of creation.

This is the psyche in its integrated state, where impulses, emotions, intellect, and instincts move in concert like a single, breathing organism.

But harmony is delicate.

Balance requires vigilance.

And even divine energies can fall out of alignment.

When an emanation grows too strong or too weak, when it separates from the others, when it forgets its place in the whole, its light flickers. It hardens. It hollows. It becomes a shell — a Qliphah. These shells are not demons in the monstrous sense. They are distortions, husks, fragments of energy that have lost their balance. They are the shadows cast by virtues when they stand alone.

This is the Devil's first teaching: shadow is not evil — it is imbalance.

Compassion without boundaries becomes suffocation — the shadow of Cups.

Strength without tenderness becomes cruelty — the shadow of Wands.

Clarity without humility becomes arrogance — the shadow of Swords.

Stability without movement becomes stagnation — the shadow of Pentacles.

Each Qliphah is a reminder that every virtue contains its own distortion.

Every strength can become a trap.

Every gift can become a cage.

The Qliphoth whisper to the psyche:

"You are only this."

"You must cling to this."

"You cannot change."

"You are defined by your fear, your desire, your certainty, your hunger."

Their voices are subtle — not shouts, but murmurs that curl around the edges of awareness. This is the Devil's illusion: the belief that we are bound by our patterns, that our distortions are our identity, that the shell is the self. But the Qliphoth are hollow. They have no life of their own. They exist only when we feed them with unconsciousness.

The work is not to destroy them, but to see them.

To recognize the imbalance.

To restore the connection.

To bring the isolated energy back into relationship with the whole.

This is the spiritual alchemy of Temperance's shadow counterpart: integration through awareness. When the psyche sees clearly, the shells crack. When the heart becomes vigilant, the distortions soften. When the mind becomes aware, the illusions dissolve. When the will becomes steady, the fragments return to harmony.

The Qliphoth teach that liberation is not achieved by fighting shadow, but by understanding it. The Devil teaches that bondage is often self-imposed. The suits teach that shadow is simply virtue bent out of shape. Together, they reveal that freedom is found through vigilance, awareness, and choice — the willingness to see where we have become unbalanced, and the courage to restore ourselves to wholeness.

Just like the Devil and the shadow suits, the Qliphoth show us that the path to liberation runs through the places where we have become fragmented. They remind us that shadow is not a punishment, but an invitation — a call to return to balance, to integration, and to the truth of who we are beneath the shell.

## Closing Reflection

The Devil presides over chained figures, reminding us that enslavement is often chosen, not imposed. The shadow suits mirror his lesson – obsession, despair, cruelty, and greed are distortions of our gifts. Together, they remind us that vigilance is the path to freedom.

Psychology shows that the mind can become attached to familiar patterns, even when they harm us. Habit loops, reward cycles, and fear responses can keep us tethered to what we've outgrown. The Devil reflects this inner architecture — the way bondage often begins with small compromises that slowly shape our perception of what is possible.

Cosmically, he echoes the gravitational pull of dense celestial bodies. Some forces draw us in not through malice, but through inertia; escape requires awareness, energy, and a deliberate change in trajectory. His chains are not absolute — they loosen the moment we recognize their weight.

And in our cultural moment — where distraction is constant and desire is easily manipulated — the Devil offers a necessary clarity. Temptation is universal. To recognize shadow, to resist bondage, and to choose light is to live with awareness and liberation — not by denying our impulses, but by reclaiming the agency to direct them.

## Journaling prompt

*What attachment, habit, or belief might be limiting your freedom, and how could you release it?*

# The Tower and the Catastrophic Moments

## Crisis, Revelation, and the Collapse of False Certainty

*"Egotistical pursuits can only take you as far as you can see. To view what lies beyond that which you know, accept that more exists than you can currently see, and allow change to bring forth a shift in awareness that transcends your current orbit."*

*– Excerpt from Tarot Well Done*

## The Tower as Number Sixteen: The Archetype of Collapse

The Tower is the sixteenth card of the Major Arcana, and the most dramatic symbol of crisis and revelation. Where Temperance taught balance and the Devil warned of shadow, the

Tower strips away illusion entirely. Lightning strikes, fire rages, and figures fall from their lofty perch. The message is clear: what is built on false foundations cannot endure.

Psychologically, the Tower reflects the stage of breakdown – moments when denial, ego, or complacency are shattered by reality. Collapse is not failure – it is the moment when a structure can no longer hold what was never true. Failure is personal; collapse is structural. Spiritually, it embodies the principle of surrender: that enlightenment often comes only after collapse. Its lesson is that destruction is not the end, but the clearing of space for truth.

## Catastrophic Moments Across the Suits

The Tower's collapse is mirrored in the Minor Arcana through cards that depict crisis in creativity, emotion, intellect, and material life. These are not gentle lessons – they are the moments when instability manifests and forces transformation.

### Wands (Fire): Creative Chaos

The fire of Wands, when destabilized, becomes chaos and burnout. The Ten of Wands shows burden; under the Tower's influence, that burden collapses into exhaustion. The lesson is that passion without moderation leads to destruction, and creative energy must be grounded to endure.

## Cups (Water): Emotional Upheaval

The water of Cups, when destabilized, becomes heartbreak and despair. The Five of Cups shows grief; under the Tower's influence, emotional structures collapse, forcing us to confront loss. The lesson is that emotional security cannot be built on denial – it must face truth to heal.

## Swords (Air): Mental Breakdown

The air of Swords, when destabilized, becomes anxiety and collapse of clarity. The Nine of Swords shows torment; under the Tower's influence, mental constructs shatter, leaving us exposed to raw truth. The lesson is that intellect alone cannot protect us from crisis – perspective must be surrendered to transformation.

## Pentacles (Earth): Material Loss

The earth of Pentacles, when destabilized, becomes financial ruin or collapse of stability. The Five of Pentacles shows poverty; under the Tower's influence, material security crumbles, reminding us that possessions are impermanent. The lesson is that true wealth lies in resilience, not accumulation.

## The Tower and the Suits Together

The Tower teaches that collapse is universal:

- ❖ **Wands (Fire):** Creative chaos.

- ❖ **Cups (Water):** Emotional upheaval.

- ❖ **Swords (Air):** Mental breakdown.

- ❖ **Pentacles (Earth):** Material loss.

Together, they remind us that crisis is not confined to one domain – it is the stripping away of false certainty across all aspects of life. The Tower's lesson is that collapse is the doorway to awakening.

## Psychological and Spiritual Resonance

From a psychological perspective, the Tower and the catastrophic suits represent the stage of surrender – learning to accept that breakdown is part of growth. They reflect the moment when a person begins to understand that collapse is not a failure of strength but a release of what can no longer support development. This psychological recognition naturally opens into the spiritual dimension, because the experience of breakdown is inseparable from the deeper truth that revelation often arrives only when old structures fall away.

From a spiritual perspective, they embody the principle of revelation: that collapse clears away illusion, not identity – what falls is the false structure, not the self. Where psychology describes how surrender forms, spirituality describes what it is for – revealing that destruction is not an ending but a clearing, a necessary space-making for truth to emerge.

The Tower reminds us that crisis is sacred. The suits remind us that collapse is practical. Together, they reveal that surrender is the path to transformation, and that every breakdown carries within it the possibility of a more honest, more aligned beginning.

## Sky Woman's Fall – American Indigenous Tradition

The story of the Tower begins in the Sky World, a realm suspended above the waters where life unfolds in luminous order. The air there is soft and bright, the ground warm beneath bare feet. The people of the Sky World move through their days with quiet certainty. They believe their home is eternal, their foundations unshakable, their way of life secure. It is a world built on the gentle assumption that what exists now will exist forever.

This is the illusion before collapse — the calm before the structure breaks.

One day, a fissure opens in the floor of the Sky World. At first it is only a hairline crack, a thin line of darkness against the glowing earth. But it widens with a force no one can stop, the ground trembling as if exhaling something long held. A woman approaches the edge, drawn by a mixture of curiosity and unease. She leans closer, and the ground beneath her gives way.

She falls. The rupture swallows her, and she plummets toward the endless waters below. The fall is sudden, irreversible, absolute. Wind rushes past her ears. Light blurs. There is nothing to grasp, nothing to slow her descent. It is the moment when the old world shatters and nothing can be held onto.

This is the Tower's essence: the collapse that reveals the truth.

As Sky Woman descends, she cannot cling to anything. There is no structure to hold, no certainty to anchor her. She must surrender to the unknown. The catastrophic moment is not a punishment but a passage — a threshold where the familiar dissolves and the future has not yet taken form. It is the surrender that comes when resistance is no longer possible.

Yet the waters below are alive with beings who see her falling. Geese rise in a flurry of wings, catching her gently, their feathers soft against her skin. Turtle swims forward, steady and ancient, offering his back as a place to land. Other animals dive into the depths, bringing up mud from the bottom of the sea. They place it on Turtle's shell, and the mud expands, warm and living, becoming the earth itself. What seemed like an ending becomes the ground for a new beginning. Collapse becomes creation.

Sky Woman carries seeds from the Sky World, held close even as she fell. She plants them in the new soil. They take root and flourish. Plants grow. Animals gather. Life emerges from the fall — not in spite of it, but because of it. The rupture in the Sky World becomes the birth of the world below. The catastrophe becomes the foundation of a new reality.

The Tower teaches that crisis is sacred because it breaks apart what was never stable. The catastrophic suits echo this truth in their own ways: the fire of Wands that burns through false momentum, the waters of Cups that flood emotional illusions, the winds of Swords that cut through false narratives, and the earth of Pentacles that crumbles structures built on fear. Each suit reveals how collapse clears space for what must come next.

Sky Woman's fall shows that when the old world breaks, a new one can be born. The Tower reminds us that surrender is not defeat but the doorway to transformation. The catastrophic suits remind us that collapse is practical, clearing away what cannot endure. Together, they reveal that revelation arrives when illusion falls — and that the ground we land on after the fall may be more fertile than the world we left behind.

## Closing Reflection

The Tower blazes with fire, its crown shattered, figures falling into the unknown. The catastrophic suits mirror its lesson —

creative chaos, emotional upheaval, mental breakdown, and material loss are the crucibles of transformation. Together, they remind us that collapse is not the end – it is the beginning of truth.

In psychology, disruption often precedes breakthrough. The mind reorganizes itself when old frameworks fail, allowing new patterns to emerge from what first feels like disorientation. The Tower reflects this inner process — the way clarity can rise from the ashes of what no longer holds.

Cosmically, it echoes the explosive deaths of stars. Supernovae look like destruction, yet they scatter the elements that make new worlds possible. Collapse becomes creation, not through comfort, but through the release of what was too dense to sustain itself.

And in our cultural moment — where instability can feel relentless and certainty is often an illusion — the Tower offers a fierce kind of honesty. Crisis is the threshold of awakening. To accept collapse, to surrender ego, and to embrace revelation is to live with courage and clarity — not by avoiding the fall, but by allowing it to reveal what is real.

## Journaling prompt

*What truth or revelation has recently shaken your foundations, and what new clarity is emerging?*

# The Star and the Healing Aspects

## Hope, Renewal, and the Return of Inspiration

*"Your inner truth is eternal and effortless. Life is hope and spiritual surrender clears the path for truth."*

*– Excerpt from Tarot Well Done*

## The Star as Number Seventeen: The Archetype of Renewal

The Star is the seventeenth card of the Major Arcana, arriving after the devastation of the Tower. Where collapse stripped away illusion, the Star restores hope. A woman kneels by water, pouring life into both pool and land, under the light of eight radiant stars. Her nakedness symbolizes rebirth – she is pure, unencumbered, and aligned with truth.

Psychologically, the Star reflects the stage of renewal – moments when despair gives way to clarity, and self-esteem is restored. Healing often begins as a subtle reorientation, a quiet shift rather than a dramatic transformation. Spiritually, it embodies the principle of inspiration: that hope is eternal, and that surrender clears the path for truth. Its lesson is that healing is possible after collapse, and that renewal is the natural rhythm of life.

## Healing Aspects Across the Suits

The Star's archetype of renewal is mirrored in the Minor Arcana through cards that depict healing, generosity, and clarity across creativity, emotion, intellect, and material life.

### Wands (Fire): Creative Renewal

The fire of Wands, when healed, becomes inspiration and vision. The Three of Wands shows anticipation of new horizons; under the Star's influence, creative energy is restored, and passion is directed toward growth.

### Cups (Water): Emotional Healing

The water of Cups, when healed, becomes compassion and joy. The Six of Cups shows nostalgia and kindness; under the Star's influence, emotional wounds soften, and relationships are renewed with generosity and love.

## Swords (Air): Mental Clarity

The air of Swords, when healed, becomes truth and perspective. The Ace of Swords shows clarity of thought; under the Star's influence, intellect is sharpened, and confusion dissolves into insight.

## Pentacles (Earth): Material Generosity

The earth of Pentacles, when healed, becomes generosity and stability. The Six of Pentacles shows sharing of wealth; under the Star's influence, material security is balanced with compassion, creating harmony between giving and receiving.

# The Star and the Suits Together

The Star teaches that healing is universal:

- **Wands (Fire):** Creative renewal.

- **Cups (Water):** Emotional healing.

- **Swords (Air):** Mental clarity.

- **Pentacles (Earth):** Material generosity.

Together, they remind us that renewal is not confined to one domain – it is the restoration of balance across all aspects of life. Renewal rarely arrives all at once – it gathers slowly. The Star's lesson is that hope is eternal, and healing is always possible.

## Psychological and Spiritual Resonance

From a psychological perspective, the Star and the healing suits represent the stage of renewal – learning to restore self-esteem, embrace generosity, and regain clarity. They reflect the moment when a person begins to understand that healing is not a sudden return to strength, but a gradual reorientation toward possibility. This psychological softening naturally opens into the spiritual dimension, because the work of renewal is inseparable from the deeper truth that inspiration arises when the inner landscape is cleared of what once obscured it.

From a spiritual perspective, they embody the principle of inspiration: that hope is eternal, and that surrender clears the path for truth. Where psychology describes how renewal forms, spirituality describes what it is for – revealing that inspiration is not an escape from difficulty, but a light that becomes visible only after collapse has made space for it.

The Star reminds us that renewal is sacred precisely because it unfolds slowly. The suits remind us that healing is practical. Together, they reveal that inspiration is the foundation of growth, and that every small act of restoration becomes a step toward a future shaped by clarity rather than fear.

# Amaterasu's Return – Japanese Shinto Tradition

The story of the Star begins in darkness. After a rupture in the heavens and a conflict that wounds her spirit, the sun goddess Amaterasu retreats into a cave, sealing herself away from the world. The entrance closes behind her like a final breath. Without her light, the earth falls into shadow. Crops wither. Rivers cool. Spirits dim. The world enters a long night — not of punishment, but of grief.

This is the moment after the Tower: the stillness that follows collapse, when the psyche cannot yet imagine renewal.

Outside the cave, the other deities gather. They do not shout or demand. They do not try to force her return. Instead, they begin to create the conditions for her healing. They polish a mirror until it gleams like captured dawn. They craft jewels that shimmer with soft, living color. They begin to dance, their feet stirring dust into gentle spirals. Their laughter rises like a spark in the darkness — not a command, but an offering. A reminder that life continues even when the heart has withdrawn.

Healing begins not with pressure, but with invitation.

Amaterasu hears the commotion and feels a flicker of curiosity — the first movement inside her since she closed herself away. She peeks out. The mirror catches her eye. For the first time since her retreat, she sees her own reflection — not as she feared she had become, but as she truly is: radiant, powerful, whole.

The sight softens her grief. Something inside her loosens. She steps forward. Light spills from the cave, washing over the world in a warm, golden wave. The earth stirs. Plants lift their heads. Spirits rise. Renewal begins.

This is the Star's essence: the return of hope after devastation, the gentle reawakening of the self, the moment when light re-enters a life that had forgotten its own brightness.

The healing suits echo this moment in their own ways.

Wands rekindle inspiration, reminding us that creativity returns in small sparks.

Cups restore emotional flow, teaching that generosity begins with the willingness to feel again.

Swords clear the mind, revealing truth after confusion.

Pentacles rebuild the body and the world, grounding healing in daily practice.

Amaterasu's emergence shows that renewal is not forced; it is allowed. It happens when the psyche is ready to see itself clearly again. It happens when the world around us offers support without demand. It happens when we remember that our light was never lost — only hidden.

The Star teaches that renewal is sacred.

The suits teach that healing is practical.

Together, they reveal that inspiration is the foundation of growth — the quiet, steady flame that guides us back to ourselves after the long night.

Just like Amaterasu stepping from the cave, the Star reminds us that healing begins with a single moment of openness, a single breath of clarity, a single glimpse of our own radiance reflected back to us. And from that moment, the world begins to shine again.

## Closing Reflection

The Star shines with radiant light, a woman pouring water into pool and land, embodying renewal and hope. The healing suits mirror her lesson – creative renewal, emotional healing, mental clarity, and material generosity are the gifts of restoration. Together, they remind us that hope is eternal, and that renewal follows collapse.

Biology shows that healing is not a single event but a gradual recalibration. The body repairs itself through cycles of rest, nourishment, and gentle activation, rebuilding strength in ways that are often invisible at first. The Star reflects this quiet process — the way restoration begins long before we feel transformed.

Cosmically, she echoes the light of distant stars that reach us across unimaginable distances. Even after a star has died, its light continues to travel, offering guidance long after its source has changed form. Hope works the same way — a signal that persists, reminding us that renewal is already on its way.

And in our cultural moment — where exhaustion is common and cynicism can feel like the safer choice — the Star offers a softer truth. Inspiration is the path to wholeness. To embrace renewal, to restore clarity, and to live with generosity is to walk in the light of truth — not by denying what has been lost, but by trusting in what can be restored.

## Journaling prompt

*Where can you invite hope, inspiration, or healing into your life right now?*

# The Moon and the Cards of Illusion

## Uncertainty, Subconscious, and the Challenge of Discernment

*"Where hope guides the way, fearfulness and doubt prevents you from seeing the path of truth."*

*— Excerpt from Tarot Well Done*

## The Moon as Number Eighteen: The Archetype of Illusion

The Moon is the eighteenth card of the Major Arcana, and the most enigmatic. Where the Star offered renewal and clarity, the Moon confronts us with illusion, confusion, and the distortions of fear. A wolf and a dog howl at an eclipse, a crayfish crawls uncertainly at the water's edge, and a narrow path winds between pillars into the unknown. The Moon's lesson is that imagination can deceive, and that discernment is required to separate truth from illusion. Intuition arises from inner alignment, while imagination under anxiety fills the gaps with stories that mislead.

Psychologically, the Moon reflects the stage of uncertainty – moments when anxiety, doubt, or self-delusion cloud judgment. Spiritually, it embodies the principle of humility: that true intuition requires surrender, not control. Its lesson is that fear and illusion are obstacles to truth, and that clarity comes only through surrender to higher consciousness.

## Illusion Across the Suits

The Moon's archetype of illusion is mirrored in the Minor Arcana through cards that depict deception, confusion, or hidden truths across creativity, emotion, intellect, and material life.

### Wands (Fire): Creative Misdirection

The fire of Wands, when distorted, becomes misdirected ambition or false inspiration. The Seven of Wands shows defense against opposition; under the Moon's influence, this defense may be based on imagined threats rather than reality. The lesson is that passion must be grounded in truth, not illusion.

## Cups (Water): Emotional Fog

The water of Cups, when distorted, becomes emotional confusion or fantasy. The Seven of Cups shows choices clouded by illusion; under the Moon's influence, desires may become deceptive, leading to disappointment. The lesson is that emotional clarity requires discernment, not indulgence.

## Swords (Air): Mental Indecision

The air of Swords, when distorted, becomes indecision or self-deception. The Two of Swords shows a blindfolded figure at a crossroads; under the Moon's influence, intellect is clouded, and choices are delayed by fear. The lesson is that truth must be faced, even when uncomfortable.

## Pentacles (Earth): Material Insecurity

The earth of Pentacles, when distorted, becomes mistrust or insecurity. The Five of Pentacles shows poverty and exclusion; under the Moon's influence, material fears may be exaggerated, obscuring opportunities for support and renewal. The lesson is that material security must be grounded in reality, not fear.

# The Moon and the Suits Together

The Moon teaches that illusion is universal:

- ❖ **Wands (Fire):** Creative misdirection.

- ❖ **Cups (Water):** Emotional fog.

- ❖ **Swords (Air):** Mental indecision.

- ❖ **Pentacles (Earth):** Material insecurity.

Together, they remind us that deception is not external alone –
it is the distortion of our own perception. The Moon's lesson is
that discernment is the path through illusion.


## Psychological and Spiritual Resonance

From a psychological perspective, the Moon and the illusion
suits represent the stage of discernment – learning to recognize
how fear and imagination distort perception. They reflect the
moment when a person begins to understand that uncertainty
amplifies whatever stories the mind is already carrying, and that
clarity requires the courage to question those stories. This
psychological vigilance naturally opens into the spiritual
dimension, because the work of naming distortion is inseparable
from the deeper truth that humility is required before intuition
can be trusted.

From a spiritual perspective, they embody the principle of
humility: that intuition requires surrender, and that truth is

found only when illusion is released. Where psychology describes how distortion forms, spirituality describes what it obscures – revealing that humility is not self-doubt, but the willingness to let go of false certainty so that deeper knowing can emerge.

The Moon reminds us that illusion is powerful. The suits remind us that deception is practical. Together, they reveal that discernment is the path to truth, and that every encounter with confusion is an invitation to slow down, soften, and see with clearer eyes.

## Ra's Night Journey – Egyptian Mythology

The story of the Moon begins at sunset, when the sun god Ra descends from the sky and enters the Duat, the realm beneath the world. In daylight, Ra is radiant, sovereign, and clear — a presence that leaves no room for doubt. But at night, he becomes a traveler in a landscape where nothing is certain. The Duat is a place of shifting forms, where shadows move with intention and the boundaries between truth and illusion dissolve.

This is the Moon's domain — the realm of intuition, ambiguity, and the soft distortions of the night-mind.

Ra travels in a sacred barque, its hull glowing faintly in the darkness. He is accompanied by deities who embody protection, insight, and perception. Together they move through winding passages, past gates guarded by beings whose faces change as one looks at them. The waters ripple with shapes that may be spirits or reflections. The air hums with whispers that may be warnings or echoes.

In the Duat, nothing is what it seems. This is the psychological landscape of the Moon — the place where projection, fear, and imagination intertwine.

At the deepest point of the journey, Ra encounters Apophis, the great serpent of chaos. Apophis is not a creature of malice but of distortion. He bends light, twists perception, and coils around the barque in an attempt to halt its passage. His presence is disorienting — a force that makes the familiar feel strange and the strange feel inevitable. Ra cannot destroy him permanently; Apophis returns every night.

This is the Moon's truth: illusion is not defeated once and for all. It must be recognized again and again, each time with greater clarity.

Ra's companions chant spells, steady their breath, and hold their focus. They do not fight chaos with force but with awareness. They see through the serpent's shifting forms. They remember what is real. Slowly, the barque moves forward. The serpent loosens. The waters calm. The night begins to thin.

At last, Ra reaches the horizon. The barque rises. Light returns to the world. Dawn breaks not because the night was conquered, but because it was navigated with vigilance and intuition.

This is the Moon's essence: the journey through illusion that leads to renewed clarity.

The suits echo this passage in their own ways.

Wands reveal how inspiration can become fantasy when untethered.

Cups show how emotion can blur into projection.

Swords expose how thought can twist into anxiety.

Pentacles remind us that even the material world can deceive when fear distorts perception.

The Moon teaches that illusion is part of the path.

The suits teach that distortion arises when one aspect of the self overwhelms the others.

Together, they reveal that clarity is born not from avoiding the night, but from learning to see within it.

Just like Ra's nightly journey, the Moon reminds us that the psyche must pass through darkness to rediscover its own light. Illusion is not a failure — it is a threshold. And when we learn to navigate it with awareness, dawn always returns.

## Closing Reflection

The Moon glows over wolf and dog, crayfish and pillars, embodying illusion and uncertainty. The suits mirror its lesson – creative misdirection, emotional fog, mental indecision, and material insecurity are the distortions of fear. Together, they remind us that discernment is the final challenge before clarity.

Neuroscience shows that fear can distort perception, narrowing our attention and amplifying imagined threats. The brain fills gaps with familiar patterns, even when those patterns mislead us. The Moon reflects this inner landscape — the way uncertainty invites projection, and how awareness begins when we question what we think we see.

Cosmically, she echoes the shifting light of lunar cycles. The moon never changes shape, yet its appearance transforms night by night, reminding us that perception is fluid. What seems hidden is often simply waiting for the right angle of illumination.

And in our cultural moment — where ambiguity is uncomfortable and quick conclusions are rewarded — the Moon offers a gentler discipline. Truth is hidden by fear. To release illusion, to surrender ego, and to walk the narrow path is to live with humility and clarity — not by demanding certainty, but by learning to see through the dim light with patience and trust.

The Moon teaches us to walk by dim light, trusting that dawn is already forming beyond the horizon.

## Journaling prompt

*What illusions or uncertainties are clouding your vision, and how might you discern what is real?*

# The Sun and the Triumphs
## Joy, Clarity, and the Radiance of Success

*"Your inner truth is eternal and effortless. Life is hope and spiritual surrender clears the path for truth."*

*– Excerpt from Tarot Well Done*

## The Sun as Number Nineteen: The Archetype of Clarity

The Sun is the nineteenth card of the Major Arcana, and the most luminous. After the Moon's illusions, the Sun restores clarity, vitality, and joy. A child rides freely on a white horse, sunflowers bloom, and the radiant sun fills the sky. The message is simple yet profound: truth is revealed, and life flourishes in its light.

Psychologically, the Sun reflects the stage of triumph — moments when confidence, clarity, and joy are restored.

Spiritually, it embodies the principle of illumination: that truth is radiant, and that vitality is the natural state of alignment. Its lesson is that joy is not frivolous – it is the sign of harmony between self and Source. The Sun reminds us that joy is not an escape from reality, but the natural radiance that emerges when the self is fully integrated.

## Triumphs Across the Suits

The Sun's archetype of clarity is mirrored in the Minor Arcana through cards that depict success, abundance, and joy across creativity, emotion, intellect, and material life.

### Wands (Fire): Creative Victory

The fire of Wands, when illuminated, becomes triumph and recognition. The Six of Wands shows victory and acclaim; under the Sun's influence, creative energy is celebrated, and passion is rewarded. The lesson is that vision, when pursued with integrity, leads to success.

### Cups (Water): Emotional Joy

The water of Cups, when illuminated, becomes love and harmony. The Ten of Cups shows family joy and fulfillment; under the Sun's influence, emotional bonds flourish, and relationships thrive. The lesson is that love, when lived authentically, brings lasting joy.

## Swords (Air): Mental Clarity

The air of Swords, when illuminated, becomes truth and insight. The Ace of Swords shows clarity of thought; under the Sun's influence, intellect is sharpened, and confusion dissolves. The lesson is that truth, when embraced, brings freedom.

## Pentacles (Earth): Material Prosperity

The earth of Pentacles, when illuminated, becomes abundance and stability. The Nine of Pentacles shows independence and prosperity; under the Sun's influence, material success is enjoyed with gratitude. The lesson is that prosperity, when grounded in wisdom, brings security and peace.

# The Sun and the Suits Together

The Sun teaches that triumph is universal:

- ❖ **Wands (Fire):** Creative victory.

- ❖ **Cups (Water):** Emotional joy.

- ❖ **Swords (Air):** Mental clarity.

- ❖ **Pentacles (Earth):** Material prosperity.

Together, they remind us that success is not confined to one domain – it is the flourishing of life in all aspects. The Sun's lesson is that clarity and joy are the natural outcomes of truth.

# Psychological and Spiritual Resonance

From a psychological perspective, the Sun and the triumph suits represent the stage of vitality – learning to embrace joy, celebrate success, and live with clarity. They reflect the moment when a person begins to understand that joy is not a distraction from the path, but evidence that the self is functioning in alignment. This psychological brightness naturally opens into the spiritual dimension, because the experience of vitality is inseparable from the deeper truth that illumination arises when fear no longer distorts perception.

From a spiritual perspective, they embody the principle of illumination: that truth is radiant, and that joy is sacred. Where psychology describes how vitality forms, spirituality describes what it reveals – showing that joy is not merely an emotion but a sign that the inner and outer worlds are resonating in harmony.

The Sun reminds us that clarity is eternal. The suits remind us that triumph is practical. Together, they reveal that joy is the sign of alignment with truth, and that living with vitality is both a blessing and a responsibility to remain open, honest, and fully present.

# Lugh's Radiance – Celtic Mythology.

The story of the Sun begins in a time of heaviness. The land lies under the shadow of the Fomorians, beings who thrive on stagnation, fear, and the dimming of human potential. Under their rule, joy becomes scarce. Creativity falters. Confidence wanes. The world forgets its own brightness.

This is the aftermath of the Moon's uncertainty – the moment when the psyche longs for clarity but cannot yet find it.

Into this dimness comes a young god named Lugh, whose very presence is a burst of light. He is called the Shining One, the Many-Skilled, the one whose brilliance cannot be contained. When he arrives at the gates of the Tuatha Dé Danann — the gods of light, artistry, and craft — he is asked what single skill he brings.

Lugh smiles and answers that he brings them all: craft, music, healing, strategy, poetry, truth. His radiance is not arrogance but alignment. He knows who he is. He knows what he carries. His confidence is clarity, not ego.

This the Sun's first teaching: joy returns when we remember our gifts.

The gods test him, but Lugh's brilliance is undeniable. He enters their court like dawn breaking after a long night. His presence alone begins to shift the balance. Where there was stagnation, movement returns. Where there was fear, courage stirs. Where there was confusion, clarity emerges.

Lugh does not conquer the darkness by force; he dissolves it by shining.

The triumph suits echo this moment.

Wands ignite with renewed inspiration, the spark that had been smothered now burning bright.

Cups overflow with emotional warmth, generosity returning as hearts open again.

Swords sharpen into truth, cutting through the fog of doubt and distortion.

Pentacles ground the triumph, turning radiance into practical success and flourishing life.

When the time comes to face the Fomorians, Lugh does not fight alone. His radiance awakens the gifts of everyone around him. The poets remember their voices. The healers remember their power. The warriors remember their courage. The artisans remember their craft. Under Lugh's light, the world remembers itself.

This is the Sun's deeper truth: illumination is contagious.

The battle is not a clash of brute force but a restoration of balance. Lugh's clarity reveals the weakness of the shadow. His joy rekindles the spirit of the people. His brilliance becomes a beacon. When the Fomorians fall, it is not because they were destroyed, but because the world no longer consents to dimness.

With the victory won, Lugh's radiance spreads across the land. Fields ripen. Music returns. Children laugh. The air itself feels lighter. The world steps into a new season of vitality.

This is the triumph of the Sun — not a fleeting moment of glory, but a sustained alignment with truth.

The Sun teaches that clarity is eternal.

The triumph suits teach that success is practical, embodied, and lived.

Together, they reveal that joy is not an indulgence but a sign of alignment — the unmistakable feeling of living in harmony with one's nature.

Just like Lugh stepping into the court of the gods, the Sun reminds us that illumination is our birthright, that joy is a sacred force, and that when we allow ourselves to shine, the world around us brightens in response.

## Closing Reflection

The Sun shines over child and horse, sunflowers and radiant sky, embodying clarity and joy. The triumph suits mirror its lesson – creative victory, emotional joy, mental clarity, and material prosperity are the gifts of illumination. Together, they remind us that success is not fleeting – it is the natural state of truth.

Biology shows that joy is not frivolous; it is a signal of coherence. When the nervous system feels safe and aligned, the body releases energy toward growth, creativity, and connection. The Sun reflects this inner radiance — the way clarity strengthens us from the inside out.

Cosmically, it echoes the literal sun that sustains life on Earth. Its light reveals, nourishes, and energizes, not through force but through steady presence. Illumination is generative; it brings things into being simply by shining on them.

And in our cultural moment — where cynicism can feel sophisticated and joy is sometimes dismissed as naïve — the Sun offers a deeper wisdom. Joy is sacred. To embrace clarity, to celebrate success, and to live with vitality is to walk in the radiance of truth — not as a fleeting high, but as a return to our most natural state.

The Sun does not create truth – it reveals what was always present beneath the shadows.

## Journaling prompt

*What brings you joy and vitality, and how can you embrace it more fully?*

# Judgement and the Collective Cards

## Awakening, Reckoning, and the Call to Renewal

*"Forgive yourself and others and you will be reborn."*

*– Excerpt from Tarot Well Done*

## Judgement as Number Twenty: The Archetype of Awakening

Judgement is the twentieth card of the Major Arcana, and the moment of awakening before the Fool's journey concludes. An angel blows a trumpet, calling people of all ages to rise from their caskets. Naked and equal, they gaze upward in awe. The message is clear: renewal comes through forgiveness, and rebirth follows reckoning.

Forgiveness is release, not reconciliation – a letting go of what binds the heart, not a return to what caused the wound. Forgiveness frees the self; it does not obligate reunion.

Psychologically, Judgement reflects the stage of awakening – moments when we assess our lives, release the past, and embrace transformation. Spiritually, it embodies the principle of rebirth: that forgiveness clears the path for renewal, and that awakening is collective, not solitary. Its lesson is that liberation comes through letting go, and that renewal is the destiny of all.

## Collective Responsibility Across the Suits

Judgement's archetype of awakening is mirrored in the Minor Arcana through cards that depict collective responsibility, legacy, and renewal across creativity, emotion, intellect, and material life. Under Judgement, forgiveness becomes a collective act – the release of old patterns, not the erasure of accountability.

### Wands (Fire): Communal Vision

The fire of Wands, when awakened, becomes shared purpose and collective action. The Three of Wands shows anticipation of new horizons; under Judgement's influence, vision expands beyond the self, becoming a communal pursuit. The lesson is that creativity flourishes when shared.

## Cups (Water): Emotional Legacy

The water of Cups, when awakened, becomes collective memory and emotional renewal. The Ten of Cups shows family joy; under Judgement's influence, emotional bonds extend into legacy, reminding us that love is communal. The lesson is that forgiveness restores harmony across generations.

## Swords (Air): Shared Truth

The air of Swords, when awakened, becomes collective clarity and justice. The Six of Swords shows transition; under Judgement's influence, intellect guides communities through reckoning, ensuring truth is faced together. The lesson is that awakening requires shared honesty.

## Pentacles (Earth): Material Continuity

The earth of Pentacles, when awakened, becomes legacy and collective prosperity. The Ten of Pentacles shows intergenerational wealth; under Judgement's influence, material success is seen as stewardship, not possession. The lesson is that prosperity must serve the collective, not just the individual.

# Judgement and the Suits Together

Judgement teaches that awakening is collective:

- ❖ **Wands (Fire):** Communal vision.

- ❖ **Cups (Water):** Emotional legacy.

- ❖ **Swords (Air):** Shared truth.

- ❖ **Pentacles (Earth):** Material continuity.

Together, they remind us that renewal is not confined to the self – it is the rebirth of community, legacy, and collective responsibility. Reckoning is not punishment; it is the moment when truth is finally seen clearly. Judgement's lesson is that forgiveness and awakening are shared experiences.

## Psychological and Spiritual Resonance

From a psychological perspective, Judgement and the collective suits represent the stage of awakening – learning to assess, forgive, and renew not only ourselves but our communities. They reflect the moment when a person begins to understand that awakening is less about becoming someone new and more about remembering what has always been true. This psychological clarity naturally opens into the spiritual dimension, because the work of awakening is inseparable from the deeper truth that renewal is a shared act, not an individual achievement.

From a spiritual perspective, the combined suits embody the principle of rebirth: that renewal is collective, and that forgiveness is the path to liberation. Where psychology describes

how awakening forms, spirituality describes what it is for —
revealing that rebirth is not a solitary transformation but a
communal one, shaped by the willingness to release what harms
and restore what connects.

Judgement reminds us that awakening is sacred. The suits
remind us that responsibility is practical. Together, they reveal
that rebirth is achieved through forgiveness and collective
renewal, and that liberation becomes possible when truth is met
with courage, compassion, and shared accountability.

## The Orishas Restore Balance – West African Mythology

The story of Judgement begins in a time when the world has
drifted out of harmony. The rivers run low, their beds cracked
and thirsty. Conflicts rise like heat from the ground.
Communities fracture into smaller and smaller pieces. The air
itself feels heavy, as though carrying the weight of everything
that has been forgotten — obligations to one another, to the
earth, to the unseen forces that sustain life.

This is not a punishment but a consequence, the natural result
of losing sight of the threads that bind all beings together.

The orishas watch from the realm of spirit. They see the
imbalance spreading like a slow shadow across the land. They do
not rush to intervene. They wait, observing, listening, discerning

the deeper cause. Judgement is never impulsive; it is a call that emerges when the truth can no longer be ignored.

At last, the orishas gather. Each arrives with a different form of wisdom.

Oshun brings compassion and sweetness, her presence softening the air.

Ogun brings strength and clarity of purpose, his footsteps steady as iron.

Obatala brings peace and justice, a calm that settles the room.

Shango brings fire and righteous truth, his energy sharp and illuminating.

And Orunmila, the orisha of destiny and insight, brings the sacred chain of Ifá — the instrument that reveals the hidden order beneath chaos.

Orunmila casts the chain. It falls with a soft clatter, the links arranging themselves into patterns that shimmer like a cosmic mirror. The truth becomes visible: the world has not been cursed or abandoned. It has simply fallen out of alignment because humans have forgotten their interconnectedness. The crisis is not divine wrath but human amnesia.

This is Judgement's first teaching: awakening begins with remembering.

The orishas descend to earth not to condemn but to call humanity back into balance. They speak through dreams, through signs, through the quiet intuition that stirs in the heart when truth approaches. They remind people of their responsibilities — to care for the land, to honor their ancestors, to treat one another with dignity, to live in harmony with the forces that sustain life.

Communities begin to gather. Old conflicts soften. Rituals are revived. Offerings are made. The rivers are tended. The land is honored. People listen to one another again. The world does not change all at once; it shifts through countless small acts of remembrance.

This is the essence of collective responsibility — the understanding that no single person can restore balance alone, but that everyone has a role in the rising.

The suits echo this awakening. Wands ignite with purpose, calling people to act with courage and integrity. Cups open with compassion, healing the fractures between hearts. Swords sharpen into truth, cutting through denial and distortion. Pentacles ground the renewal, turning intention into embodied practice.

Judgement is not the end of the story but the moment when the world inhales again after a long silence. It is the collective rising, the shared recognition that we belong to one another, that our choices shape the whole, that truth is not a burden but a liberation.

The orishas do not restore balance for humanity; they restore balance with humanity. The awakening is mutual. The responsibility is shared. The transformation is communal.

Judgement teaches that awakening is sacred.

The suits teach that responsibility is practical.

Together, they reveal that truth is not a verdict but a call — a summons to rise, to remember, and to participate in the healing of the world.

Just like the orishas casting the chain of Ifá, Judgement reminds us that clarity arrives when we are ready to see, and that the world is renewed when we answer the call together. The orishas do not demand perfection; they call for participation.

## Closing Reflection

Judgment resounds with trumpet and angel, people rising from caskets, embodying awakening and rebirth. The collective suits mirror its lesson – communal vision, emotional legacy, shared truth, and material continuity are the gifts of renewal. Together, they remind us that awakening is not solitary – it is collective.

Psychology shows that transformation deepens when it is witnessed. Shared narratives, communal repair, and collective meaning-making strengthen the neural pathways that support lasting change. Judgement reflects this truth — that rebirth is amplified when it happens in connection, not isolation.

Cosmically, it echoes the resonance found throughout the universe. Waves, particles, and even galaxies influence one another across vast distances; nothing evolves alone. The trumpet's call symbolizes this universal principle — a signal that awakens not just the individual, but the whole.

And in our cultural moment — where fragmentation is common and unity can feel fragile — Judgement offers a restorative vision. Forgiveness is the path to rebirth. To release the past, to embrace renewal, and to awaken together is to live with freedom and grace — not as separate beings, but as participants in a shared rising. Forgiveness releases space previously weighted down by the past, so that awakening can take root in its place.

## Journaling prompt

*What awakening or call to action is stirring within you, and how will you respond?*

# The World and the Deck Synthesis

## Completion, Integration, and the Elevation of the Journey

*"Pause for a moment to celebrate your success because the moment you step forward a new journey shall begin."*

*– Excerpt from Tarot Well Done*

## The World as Number Twenty-One: The Archetype of Wholeness

The World is the twenty-first card of the Major Arcana, and the final stage of the Fool's journey. A figure floats within a laurel wreath, holding two wands, surrounded by the four evangelists. It is the image of completion, integration, and unity. The Fool has traversed innocence, will, wisdom, love, courage, shadow, collapse, renewal, and awakening. Now, all lessons are synthesized into wholeness.

Psychologically, the World reflects the stage of integration – moments when all aspects of self are unified, and identity is complete. Spiritually, it embodies the principle of continuity: that life is cyclical, and that completion is always the threshold of new beginnings. Its lesson is that wholeness is achieved not by perfection, but by integration of all experiences. Integration is not the absence of contradiction, nor is it perfection. It is the willingness to include every part of the self.

## Synthesis Across the Suits

The World's archetype of completion is mirrored in the Minor Arcana not by a single number, but by the entire deck. Each suit contributes to the synthesis, showing how creativity, emotion, intellect, and material life are integrated into wholeness.

### Wands (Fire): Creative Fulfillment

The fire of Wands culminates in vision realized. Projects are completed, passions are integrated, and creativity is harnessed into legacy. The lesson is that inspiration finds its fulfillment in contribution.

### Cups (Water): Emotional Harmony

The water of Cups culminates in love sustained. Relationships are healed, bonds are deepened, and emotional wisdom is integrated into community. The lesson is that compassion finds its fulfillment in connection.

## Swords (Air): Intellectual Clarity

The air of Swords culminates in truth embraced. Ideas are tested, illusions dispelled, and intellect is integrated into discernment. The lesson is that clarity finds its fulfillment in wisdom.

## Pentacles (Earth): Material Continuity

The earth of Pentacles culminates in prosperity shared. Wealth is stewarded, resources are sustained, and material life is integrated into legacy. The lesson is that abundance finds its fulfillment in continuity.

# The World and the Suits Together

The World teaches that completion is universal:

- **Wands (Fire):** Creative fulfillment.

- **Cups (Water):** Emotional harmony.

- **Swords (Air):** Intellectual clarity.

- **Pentacles (Earth):** Material continuity.

Together, they remind us that wholeness is not confined to one domain – it is the integration of all. The World's lesson is that completion is the synthesis of creativity, emotion, intellect, and material life. To integrate is to weave together, the self, the world, the inner truth, and the outer participation.

## Psychological and Spiritual Resonance

From a psychological perspective, the World and the deck synthesis represent the stage of integration – learning to unify all aspects of self, and to embrace continuity. They reflect the moment when a person begins to understand that integration is not a final achievement but an ongoing capacity to hold complexity without fragmentation. This psychological coherence naturally opens into the spiritual dimension, because the work of integration is inseparable from the deeper truth that wholeness includes every part of the self, even what once felt unbearable.

From a spiritual perspective, they embody the principle of wholeness: that completion is sacred, and that every ending is the beginning of a new cycle. Where psychology describes how integration forms, spirituality describes what it participates in – revealing that wholeness is not perfection but the willingness to include shadow and light, past and future, self and world in a single, continuous rhythm.

The World reminds us that integration is eternal. The suits remind us that synthesis is practical. Together, they reveal that wholeness is achieved through unity and continuity, and that every cycle of completion becomes the doorway through which the next chapter of becoming begins.

## Churning the Ocean of Milk – Hindu Tradition

The story of the World begins not with triumph, but with weariness. The gods are tired. Their strength has thinned. Their radiance has dimmed. Even their joy feels distant, like a memory they can't quite touch. The world is still turning, but something essential has slipped out of place.

They gather at the edge of the cosmic ocean — the Ocean of Milk — and stare into its endless surface. They know they cannot restore themselves alone. They know they must ask for help from those they once called enemies. This is the moment of humility before integration, the moment when the self realizes it cannot heal by dividing itself.

The asuras arrive. They are wary, proud, wounded in their own ways. But they, too, feel the imbalance. They, too, have lost something. And so, for the first time in ages, gods and asuras stand side by side, not as rivals but as beings who share the same world, the same exhaustion, the same longing for renewal.

They uproot Mount Mandara to use as a churning rod. They wrap the great serpent Vasuki around it like a rope. They take opposite ends. They look at one another — not with trust, not yet, but with recognition. They begin to pull.

The mountain turns. The ocean heaves. The serpent strains. The gods pull. The asuras pull. The world groans under the effort.

This is the work of integration — slow, repetitive, uncomfortable, necessary. The kind of work that asks everything of you and gives nothing back at first.

From the depths, treasures begin to rise.

A moon, pale and luminous.

A goddess, radiant with abundance.

Creatures of beauty and wonder.

Healing herbs.

Sacred beings.

Gifts no one expected.

But then the poison comes.

A dark, burning venom rises from the ocean — so potent it could destroy everything. The gods recoil. The asuras step back. For a moment, the churning stops. This is the shadow that emerges when the self begins to integrate — the old pain, the old fear, the old wound rising to the surface.

Shiva steps forward. He gathers the poison in his hands. He drinks it to protect the world. His throat turns blue, but he remains steady. This is the moment when the self learns that shadow is not an enemy but a truth that must be held with courage.

The churning continues.

At last, after ages of effort, the nectar of immortality rises — not in a blaze of glory, but like a quiet dawn. The gods drink. Their strength returns. Their radiance brightens. The world steadies. The cycle renews.

But something deeper has changed.

The gods and asuras look at one another differently now. They have shared the labor. They have endured the poison. They have witnessed the rising of wonders. They have participated in the renewal of the world. They have become part of one another's story.

This is the World's deepest truth: wholeness is not perfection — it is participation.

The suits echo this truth.

Wands in the pulling.

Cups in the cooperation.

Swords in the courage to face the poison.

Pentacles in the steady turning of the mountain.

The World teaches that integration is eternal — a cycle of churning, revealing, releasing, and renewing.

The suits teach that synthesis is practical — lived through effort, connection, clarity, and embodiment.

Together, they reveal that wholeness is not a destination but a rhythm — the ongoing willingness to meet every part of oneself, to work with it, to rise with it, to begin again.

Just like the gods and asuras at the edge of the cosmic ocean, The World reminds us that unity is born from the meeting of opposites, that continuity is sustained through cooperation, and that the nectar of truth rises only when the whole self is engaged.

## Closing Reflection

The World floats within laurel wreath, wands in hand, evangelists in cloud, embodying completion and wholeness. The suits mirror its lesson – creative fulfillment, emotional harmony, intellectual clarity, and material continuity are the gifts of synthesis. Together, they remind us that completion is not final – it is the threshold of renewal.

Biology shows that integration is the hallmark of a healthy system. The brain weaves experience into coherent networks, allowing past learning to support future growth. The World reflects this inner synthesis — the way wholeness emerges when disparate parts finally speak to one another.

Cosmically, she echoes the cycles of planets and galaxies, each completing vast orbits only to begin them again. Completion is never an ending; it is a return, a moment of alignment before the next movement begins. Her laurel wreath is both a crown and a doorway.

And in our cultural moment — where achievement is often treated as a finish line — the World offers a deeper truth. Wholeness is sacred. To celebrate completion, to embrace integration, and to step into renewal is to live with unity and grace — not by clinging to the final moment, but by recognizing it as the beginning of a new, expansive cycle.

## Journaling prompt

*What completion or integration in your life deserves celebration, and how will you honor it before beginning anew?*

# Reflections

## Integration, Renewal, and the Continuity of the Journey

*"A humble openness to receive is the way to universal truth."*

*– Excerpt from Tarot Well Done*

## The Fool's Journey Completed

The Fool has walked the path from innocence to mastery, from collapse to renewal, from shadow to light. Each card has revealed a stage of human development, a virtue to embody, or a challenge to overcome. The World marks the culmination of this journey: integration, wholeness, and the readiness to begin again.

Yet completion is never final. The tarot reminds us that endings are thresholds, and that every cycle of growth opens into another. The Fool's journey is eternal, and so is ours.

# Tarot as a Map of Human Development

Throughout this book, tarot has been shown not as fortune-telling, but as a symbolic language of growth. Each archetype mirrors a psychological stage:

- ❖ Strength teaches emotional regulation.

- ❖ Temperance teaches the work of integration.

- ❖ The Devil teaches shadow work.

- ❖ The Tower teaches surrender.

- ❖ The Star teaches renewal.

- ❖ The Moon teaches discernment.

- ❖ The Sun teaches vitality.

- ❖ Judgement teaches collective responsibility.

- ❖ The World teaches the completion of integration.

Temperance is the alchemy of integration; The World is the coherence that integration makes possible. One is the process, the other the culmination.

Together, the cards form a map of individuation – a path toward wholeness that is both mythic and practical.

# The Lenses of Interpretation

Throughout this book, each archetype has been explored through three interwoven lenses: the psychological, the cosmic, and the cultural. These perspectives were not added for ornament – they reveal the depth of the tarot's symbolic language.

- ❖ The psychological lens shows how each card mirrors the inner workings of the mind: regulation, shadow, resilience, insight, and integration.

- ❖ The cosmic lens reminds us that human growth follows the same principles that govern nature and the universe: cycles, equilibrium, collapse, renewal, and emergence.

- ❖ The cultural lens grounds the archetypes in the world we live in now, revealing how ancient patterns continue to shape our collective moment.

Together, these lenses illuminate the tarot as a living system that bridges inner experience, natural law, and the evolving story of humanity. They allow the Fool's journey to be known not only as myth, but as psychology, ecology, and cultural truth.

# Wisdom Beyond Tarot

The tarot is one language of growth, but it is not the only one. Across cultures and traditions, wisdom has always pointed toward the same truths: that individuation requires courage, that shadow must be faced, that collapse precedes renewal, and that wholeness is the destiny of all.

- ❖ **Jungian psychology** speaks of individuation – the integration of conscious and unconscious, mirrored in the Fool's journey.

- ❖ **Philosophers of presence** remind us that enoughness is found in being, not in striving, echoing the serenity of the Star.

- ❖ **Spiritual survival practices** teach us to break cycles of distraction and reclaim attention, resonating with the Tower's call to surrender.

- ❖ **Prophecies and ancient traditions** speak of collective awakening, mirrored in Judgement's call to renewal.

- ❖ **Spiritual psychology** emphasizes compassion with boundaries, authenticity without performance, and sensitivity as power – all lessons embedded in the suits.

- ❖ **Meditative practices** remind us that unity is not abstract, but embodied in breath, silence, and awareness – the World's integration lived in daily life.

# God Favors the Fool

At the heart of this journey lies the premise that shaped this book from the beginning: God favors the Fool.

Not God as a distant ruler or a figure in the sky, but God as the creative intelligence within us – the part of human consciousness capable of vision, courage, and renewal. The Fool is favored because the Fool is willing to cross thresholds. Willing to leave the familiar. Willing to risk misunderstanding, discomfort, and change.

The Fool steps forward not because he knows the path, but because he trusts the spark that calls him toward it. That spark is what many traditions have named God: the inner force that remembers what we are capable of becoming. It is the imagination that shapes futures, the intuition that guides us toward alignment, the quiet knowing that we are participants in creation rather than spectators of it.

To say that God favors the Fool is to say that life responds to courage. That the universe bends toward those who dare to grow. That the act of stepping forward – into uncertainty, into possibility – is itself a form of invocation.

When we remember who we are, we remember that we are not separate from the intelligence that shapes the world. We are expressions of it. Co-creators with it. The Fool is the one who lives from that truth, and in doing so, becomes a catalyst for personal and collective transformation.

## Emerging Themes

As humanity evolves, new themes continue to arise – ones already appearing in the conversations we have with each other, whether or not we realize it:

- ❖ The challenge of overstimulation and meaning-loss, and the need for silence and reflection.

- ❖ The manipulation of fear and outrage, and the importance of discernment and resilience.

- ❖ The rediscovery of authenticity, and the courage to live without masks.

- ❖ The recognition of sensitivity as strength, and intuition as a guide.

- ❖ The movement from partisan division toward collective responsibility and shared renewal.

These themes are not separate from tarot – they are its living continuation. The archetypes of the cards are alive in our world, speaking through psychology, philosophy, prophecy, and daily practice.

## Psychological and Spiritual Resonance

From a psychological perspective, the Fool's journey and these broader wisdoms converge into a single path: individuation, resilience, and authenticity. From a spiritual perspective, they embody the principle of continuity: that life is cyclical, that wholeness is eternal, and that renewal is always possible. Together, these perspectives reveal that the Fool's journey is not only the story of each card, but the story of a life – a pattern that repeats across seasons, identities, and generations.

Tarot provides the archetypal map. Spiritual psychology provides the practical tools. Wisdom traditions provide the collective memory. Together, they teach that growth is universal, and that the path is always before us.

## How to Continue the Journey

To continue the journey is to walk with the archetypes rather than merely remember them. The tarot becomes a living companion — a way of noticing where you are in the cycle, of recognizing when you are in the Hermit's solitude, the Chariot's direction, the Moon's uncertainty, or the Sun's clarity. Growth unfolds through ordinary choices: pausing before reacting, choosing truth over fear, tending to your inner world with patience. The language of tarot grows as you grow; each return to the cards reveals a new layer of yourself, a new stage of consciousness unfolding.

It is equally important to remember that the journey does not end within the self. It continues in the spaces between you and others, in the ways you participate in community, in the courage to bring your clarity into relationship. The archetypes come alive in conversation, in conflict, in collaboration – Judgement calling you toward shared responsibility, the World inviting you into continuity, the Fool asking you to meet others with openness and humility. Illumination becomes contagious. Integration becomes relational. The path continues each time you choose awareness, compassion, and courage not only for yourself, but for the world you help shape. Each step you take shapes not only your inner world but the future you help create; consciousness is participatory, and the Fool reminds us that we are co-authors of what comes next.

## Closing Reflection

The World completes the Fool's journey, but it is not the end. It is the pause before renewal, the celebration before the next step. Tarot teaches that endings are beginnings, that collapse is renewal, that shadow is the doorway to light, and that wholeness is simply the moment before the next becoming.

The wisdom of prophets, psychologists, mystics, and storytellers all converge here: individuation is eternal, and the path is always before us. And now you stand where the Fool stands — at the edge of what has been integrated, with the wind rising at your back. The pattern that renews itself through those who dare to begin again is already favoring you.

Pause to celebrate, then step forward. The journey begins again, and this time, you carry the full spectrum of human potential as your companion. Go forth and spark.

# Epilogue

## Gratitude to Pamela Colman Smith

Dear Pamela,

As I bring this book to its close, I find myself turning not to the future, but to you. My journey into tarot began with curiosity, but it deepened into transformation. What started as an enquiry into the cards became years of analysis, reflection, and research. Along the way, I discovered you — the artist whose vision gave form to the Rider-Waite deck, and whose name, for nearly a century, was hidden in the shadows of history.

It took approximately one hundred years for the world to acknowledge you as the creator of the imagery that has guided millions. Your absence from the story was never a reflection of your worth, only of the world's inability to see you clearly at the time. I dedicated my first book, *Tarot Well Done*, to you, but the delay in acknowledgment — one that goes deeper than recognizing your artistry alone — makes my gratitude feel all the more urgent and deserving of something more meaningful than a single line of thanks.

Through my study of tarot, I came to understand that your work was not simply illustration. It was translation. You took the complexities of human growth and ascension — the Fool's journey, the archetypes of consciousness — and rendered them in a language of line, color, and form. With so few colors, and with such remarkable consistency, you gave us a visual vocabulary that speaks across cultures and generations.

You painted from a place beyond instruction — from intuition, from vision, from the quiet knowing that symbols speak where words cannot. You distilled the vastness of human experience into images that are both simple and inexhaustible. That act required not only artistic skill, but profound personal awareness. You saw what others could not, and you gave it shape so that we might see ourselves.

For me, your work has been a mirror and a map. It has guided me through my own transformation, reminding me that tarot is not about prediction but about presence. It is about seeing the patterns of growth, the cycles of collapse and renewal, the shadows that lead us to light. Your art has taught me that wisdom can be carried in simplicity, that truth can be spoken in silence, and that the deepest journeys are often the quietest.

And so, I thank you — not only for the images themselves, but for the serenity they invite. In a world overflowing with distractions, your cards bring us back to ourselves. They remind us of the depth of our capabilities, the infinite ways in which we can grow, and the quiet power of knowing who we are. They show us that healing is possible — of the world, of each other, and of ourselves — if we are willing to follow the guidance you gave us.

Pamela, you favored the Fool long before the world favored you. And in doing so, you gave us a gift that continues to unfold, generation after generation. Your work continues to turn the wheel, guiding every seeker who steps onto the path. For that, and for all that your art has awakened in me, I offer my deepest gratitude.

With reverence,
Elena

# A Note

## To the Collective

*"If you get things wrong, just remember that being human means not being perfect.*
*Next time is another opportunity."*

*– Excerpt from Tarot Well Done*

# Other Titles
## by Elena Olympia Collins

*Tarot Well Done*

*Truth Lies in Twilight: The Prophecy*

**Forthcoming**

Elena is currently at work on her fourth book.

www.ingramcontent.com/pod-product-compliance
Lightning Source LLC
Chambersburg PA
CBHW051758050726
47598CB00006B/2336